Nobody Nowhere

Donna Williams

Bettye Ehman

Holding Time

How to Eliminate Conflict, Temper Tantrums, and Sibling Rivalry and Raise Happy, Loving, Successful Children

BY MARTHA G. WELCH M.D.

PHOTOGRAPHY BY
MARY ELLEN MARK

A FIRESIDE BOOK
Published by Simon &
Schuster Inc. ▪ New York
London Toronto Sydney
Tokyo

Fireside
Simon & Schuster Building
Rockefeller Center
1230 Avenue of the Americas
New York, New York 10020

First Fireside Edition, October 1989

FIRESIDE and colophon are registered trademarks
of Simon & Schuster Inc.

Designed by Liney Li
Manufactured in the United States of America

10 9 8 7 6 5 4 3 2 1
10 9 8 7 6 5 4 3 2 1 Pbk.

Library of Congress Cataloging-in-Publication Data
Welch, Martha G.
   Holding time: how to eliminate conflict, temper tantrums, and sibling
rivalry and raise happy, loving, successful children / by Martha G. Welch;
photography by Mary Ellen Mark.
      p.   cm.
   Bibliography: p.
   Includes index.
   1. Discipline of children.   2. Mother and child.   3. Child
rearing.   4. Hugging.   I. Title.
HQ7770.4W45   1988
649'.1—dc19   88-13083
                                                                          CIP

ISBN 0-671-65918-9
ISBN 0-671-68878-2 Pbk.

Holding Time is a resource book for parents. If there is a
question regarding a child's health, well-being, or development,
parents should consult a pediatrician. *Holding time,* when
practiced the way it is described in this book, increases parent-
child communication, understanding, and attachment and
should be done only by the loving, caring parents of the child.

To my family and Zack

CONTENTS

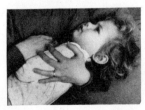

FOREWORD
BY NIKO TINBERGEN

Recipient 1973 Nobel Prize in Physiology/Medicine

HOLDING THERAPY AND PREVENTION

Since Dr. Martha Welch invented and began to apply holding time as a therapy for Early Childhood Autism, the method has been applied by a growing number of European and New World therapists. These therapists, unfortunately still largely ignored by the psychiatric profession, are now building up an impressive body of data on the favourable long-term effects of this therapy. These results show that, if practised in the correct way, holding works extraordinarily well for normal children as well as autistic children, and thus can cure a wide variety of "derailments" of human behavior development, even such common problems as tantrums, sibling rivalry, and the like. It is hoped that the treatment will now at last be acknowledged and practised on a far wider scale. Since it begins to be clear that the success is most striking when the treatment is started early in a child's life, the idea that holding can act in a preventative way begins to gain plausibility. It is already well known that the basic premise of this method grows from the natural impulses of maternity, for of course normal babies receive a version of this holding treatment as a natural matter of course in the early weeks and months of infancy.

Oxford, Spring 1988

PART ONE

The Elements of *Holding Time*

1.

IN THE BEGINNING

What Is Holding Time?

*H*olding time is a practical way for you as a mother to achieve a closer, more satisfying, and truly wonderful relationship with your child, whether your youngster is a baby in the first months of life or a toddler or a child in school.

If you are at home full-time, you may be frustrated by the feeling that giving all you have still doesn't seem to be enough. If you work, you may be concerned about your child's care or feel frustrated that you can't find more time to devote to your child. You may even be feeling guilty that you are relieved to be away from him. Whether your child-rearing problems are major or minor, or seemingly nonexistent, I believe *Holding Time* will be a revelation to you.

I have been working with mothers just like yourself at the Mothering Center in Greenwich, Connecticut, which I founded in 1978, but the evolution of the techniques explained in this book did not begin with relatively normal, sometimes demanding, often loving, frequently angry, tearful, or enthusiastic children like yours and mine. It began at the Albert Einstein College of Medicine when I was a training fellow in child psychiatry working with autistic children.

The chances of evoking a direct emotional and meaningful response from autistic children traditionally have been almost nil, notwithstanding the extraordinarily rare exceptions. But the breakthroughs that I was able to achieve and replicate were surprisingly consistent and significantly frequent. My account of those early successes was published in Nobel laureate Niko Tinbergen's book *Autistic Children, New Hope for a Cure.* It was only after those successes that I realized that the very same techniques could help a wide range of parent-child relationships.

I call the basic technique *holding time.* It is not simply a variation on a weekend at Esalen or on the touchy-feely, humanistic psychology movement of the sixties, and it is not just hugging. It is a specific, systematic technique that grew out of my training at Albert Einstein. At that time, I was working with a seriously disturbed family with a long history of disruptions in the mother-child relationships. As small children both the grandmother and the mother had spent long periods in the care of aunts. Quite by chance the mother mentioned that she had never been held as a child and that, in fact, she had not been able to bring herself to hold or cuddle her son when he was a baby. The result was that he screamed and cried endlessly for most of the first eight months, then suddenly went into autistic withdrawal. Not long after telling me this, the mother brought a Mother's Day present to the grandmother. The grandmother was so surprised and thrilled at the unexpected gift that she grabbed the mother and held her, spilling out the pent-up feelings of love and affection that she previously had not been able to express.

The mother later told me that at that moment she had wanted her mother to let go immediately and at the same time never to let go. After this single dramatic moment of longed-for contact with the grandmother, the mother's ability to respond lovingly to her child increased. Within a few days, the child's behavior dramatically improved. He became more tractable and made much better eye contact with his mother and other people—a key sign of improvement in autistic children.

Following up on this dramatic occurrence, I decided to experiment and ask the clinic mothers in my care to hold their autistic children, forcibly if necessary. The children did not want to be held. They fought and kicked, spat and bit, screamed and cried. The first patient to be held, an uncommunicative three-and-a-half-year-old named Matt, carried on for over an hour but finally calmed down. He had never been really calm before. In treatment, his mother held him daily for six weeks, and each time her son went through the same sequence: fighting and resisting, followed by calming and relating. Then one day this child—who had never said a single articulate word—looked straight at his mother during his therapy session and said, "Thank you for holding." Of course I felt sure I was on the right track.

I theorized that developmental problems of children might well be caused by a break or disturbance in the mother-child attachment or bonding process, and that systematic and protracted holding might, in fact, repair that relationship. Fortuitously, the first three patients that I treated with this technique all responded in the same year. In time, little Matt progressed to become a normal teenager with exceptional promise as a cartoonist and playwright.

Next I went on to treat other disturbed children with mother-child *holding* as an adjunct to therapy. I saw how hurt and rejected the mothers of these unresponsive children felt. A mother invariably takes personally the child's refusal to make eye contact, to speak to her, or to acknowledge her. This is especially true of mothers of autistic children, for the children respond more to other people than they do to their own mothers. The child's destructive behaviors are no less upsetting to those parents who are led by experts to think that the disorder is chemical or genetic or physiological and therefore not the parents' fault. The destructiveness can be terrifying. When, for example, an autistic son bites off a mother's nose while she sleeps, it is hard for the parents to believe that no malice was intended.

Observing these rejected mothers, I came to understand their feelings about the worst possible situation—receiving either a consistently negative response from a child or none at all.

In talking about this work with some of my friends who have children, I realized that all mothers feel like these truly rejected mothers at least *some of the time.* All children reject their mothers *some of the time.* All children have negative responses *some of the time.* My friends suggested that I teach them what I was learning about attachment for the benefit of their normal children who gave them trouble occasionally, but at that juncture I was too engrossed in my hospital work with disturbed children. Later, after I had witnessed repeated proof that *holding* can have a dramatic effect, not only on mother-child attachment but on the child's entire development, I began to use the technique with normal children with the same happy results. These successes came as a surprise to me, almost as great a surprise as the results with problem children. The levels of intimacy and expressiveness the normal children reached astonished me. I hadn't dreamed such results were possible. I had assumed that the various "norms," such as the "terrible twos," sibling rivalry, or teen rebellion, were routine and unavoidable. When they began to disappear from children who were being exposed to my technique regularly, I began to formulate a new idea of child development. The final result of this remarkable lesson is a new child-rearing philosophy. *Holding time* is, of course, a tool, a straightforward method for establishing a strong attachment or bond between a mother and a child. But this book does not merely outline a technique. It also gives you a framework for a practical philosophy of child rearing based on your own experience. As you use *holding time* to strengthen your attachment with each child, you will develop a way of life and theory of your own that will change your way of dealing with your children for the better and give you a more satisfying and more rewarding relationship with them; your children, in turn, will be more loving, happy, and successful.

One example: the mother of Lisa, age eight, was puzzled because no matter how much attention she gave her daughter, it never seemed enough. She felt that she had devoted every ounce of energy to Lisa's well-being during all of Lisa's eight years. After a course in *holding time,* Lisa's mother instituted a daily program for both her children. After some months, Lisa no longer demanded so much attention. She was much easier to be with. She began to get along beautifully with her younger brother. She was now usually thoughtful and helpful. The younger brother, who had been fearful and clinging, became confident and independent. The amount of communication of feeling among family members increased dramatically. These children, who would have been classified as normal by anyone's evaluation, became outstanding in many ways. *Holding* gave them a secure base and helped ensure their excellent development, which continued *even after their mother died three years later.*

I have many examples of normal families who profited from *holding time,* families who successfully solved a wide variety of problems from temper tantrums to whining, from drug and alcohol abuse to accident-prone behavior.

Often people wonder if holding older children will make them weak and dependent. I have found that just the opposite is true. The secure attachment attained leads to high self-esteem, high-level function, and an ability to engage in interdependent relationships.

My experience has demonstrated that after a routine of daily *holding* is established, new degrees of family cohesion and warmth are attained. The child is able to verbalize inner distress without difficulty. Parents describe feeling astonished to learn what their children have been bottling up inside. For example, after several weeks of *holding,* which led to deep and open communication, a ten-year-old felt free to tell her mother that her piano teacher had been verbally abusing her for two years.

Holding is a special experience between mother and child during which the mother excludes all other distractions while she physically embraces her child. It is a period of intense physical and emotional contact. It is surprising that all children, even relatively well-adjusted, normal children, at first respond in the same way as autistic children, becoming angry and rejecting the mother. However, normal children often resolve their anger faster and more completely than their disturbed counterparts. The resolutions almost always follow the same course: complete relaxation; open, loving communication; and tender caressing. Almost all mothers report another common reaction as well: feelings of special closeness with their child similar to feelings they had toward the child in early infancy.

The changes brought about are surprising, especially to mothers who thought things were as good as they could be. If you have an office at home or try to do any kind of work and have found it virtually impossible except when your child is napping or out of the house, then you will be pleased by the following results:

A clinging child will be less demanding or anxious.

Your child will have more self-confidence, curiosity, and motivation.

You will find less need for punishment or threats to control behavior.

Your child will show an interest in your feelings about accomplishing your work and will help by playing independently alongside you or, if older, by helping directly.

Your child will show more affection for you.

Your child will show less sibling rivalry, and you will spend less time resolving battles.

In 1978, with the volunteer aid and support of a few dedicated friends and some of the parents who wanted to undertake *holding time,* I established the Mothering Center, a nonprofit clinic for mothers and children. At the center, *holding* as a part of therapy has consistently lived up to its early promises. As a result, my main efforts of the past several years have been aimed at spreading the Welch method of *holding* therapy as an effective treatment for childhood disturbances ranging from the mildest to the most severe. Thanks to the Mothering Center's success as a demonstration laboratory, the method has been catching on. My results have been replicated by other professionals in the United States and in Europe.

Ironically, it is therapists who have worked hardest to convince us that some amount of frustration, anger, and aggression in parent-child relationships is normal. At the very least, however, the aggression is excessive and to a large degree unnecessary. Alternatives for dramatic improvement exist. These alternatives require no financial expense, no ongoing visits to therapists; in fact they are totally under your control, and you can begin to exercise them today.

The following poem by Katy, one of my brilliant ten-year-old patients, sums up in a remarkable way the effects of mother-child *holding:*

hard holding

hard holding is murder
it kills the silent army of
life destroyers
fears are faced in a confrontative
manner and reality conquers

anger is expressed in a physical
      battle making it alive and
      killable
frustrations attack frustrations
      again and again
sometimes there is a jailbreak
      before the correction
      is complete
sometimes the jailer falls
      asleep or is distracted
freedom during these times
      is not true freedom
      because the burden of
pain and isolation is
      carried by the prisoner
my jailer is persistent and
      very seldom off my case
her concentration is hard on
      the eardrums but it
      keeps me alive
sometimes she scares the words
      right out of me
control is lost
      adrenaline-charged limbs
      entangle
tears flood the battlefield
      fighters become lovers
an air of peace and love
      and connection remains
the day's activities become
      three-dimensional with
      connective depth
      a new addition
holding has saved my
      sanity and given me
      a chance to be free
      and love in a real
      growing way.
I need it and sometimes
      I want it

Let me take a moment now to describe just how this technique is used. The child is held in a position that allows the parent to make direct eye contact while controlling the child's attempts to protest, to struggle, and to escape. The technique anticipates and indeed facilitates confrontation so that problems can be resolved. I have found that the responses of parent and child in *holding* usually go through a specific sequence:

1. Confrontation

2. Rejection

3. Resolution

The mother sits in a comfortable place with her child straddling her lap, face-to-face, maximizing their awareness of each other. The child's legs are wrapped around her waist. His arms, under hers, are around her back.

The child may protest at once, or there may be several minutes of happy interchange. As the child's own emotions are aroused, the child struggles to turn away. *The mother expresses verbally her feelings*—concerns, frustrations, hope, anger, as well as affection and love—to the child. She uses her strength and tenacity to intensify the contact and prevent withdrawal. The struggle becomes desperate for both, and then, if the mother perseveres throughout the child's rejection, it dissolves into tender intimacy with intense eye contact, exploratory touching usually of the mother's face, and gentle conversation highly gratifying to both mother and child. As the sessions are repeated, increasingly secure attachment grows between them and serves as a foundation for growth in other areas of the child's overall development. The effect on the mother is also profound. Her self-esteem grows, and her capacity to cope increases. Most important, her enjoyment of her child reaches higher levels. The increase in the child's well-being in turn affects the father, whose support and active participation can greatly strengthen the results.

This is the basic technique by which mothers will find they can prevent potential problems and solve already existing difficulties. In fact, *holding time* will become indispensable to any mother who wishes to raise healthy, happy, successful children who are capable of loving others. And in the process it will enhance the loving relationship between parents and child. Everyone can benefit, and you can start right now.

2.

WHY IS *HOLDING TIME* NECESSARY?

Are the Benefits Worth the Effort?

While *holding time* is a practical technique that can change you, your child, and your relationship for the better, it is not simple or easy to do well. First let's consider why it is necessary.

Normal development occurs in a social context, which for a newborn is the mother-child relationship. The child's optimal development is most likely to take place if there is a secure bond or attachment between mother and child. This attachment develops when the mother responds sensitively to the child's needs and when the child finds that its own attempts at communication succeed in eliciting a satisfying response. Without this responsiveness, the bond will be impaired and problems may develop. Involved here are not only the personalities and styles of both mother and child but also any physical or psychological stresses that may occur while they are establishing their relationship. Failure to achieve optimal attachment, then, is not necessarily anyone's fault but is more likely a result of a combination of circumstances—anything from the mother's or the child's hospitalization to a death in the family. It is clear from my work with mothers and children that problems of attachment can arise at any time in development, not just early in life, and such problems are very common. Fortunately, the problems of bonding can be resolved, or at least improved, at any time.

The degree of attachment or bonding may range from very secure at one end of the spectrum to failed at the other. Thus there are the fortunate children who never suffer any disruptions but who are responsive from the start and who continue to have a good ongoing relationship or attachment to their mothers. What is most notable in such children is not only a strikingly successful physical and mental development but a profound capacity for relating to another person in a mutually gratifying way. This capacity for mutuality includes all relationships, not solely that with the mother. How, then, can a mother enhance this capacity? How can a mother achieve harmony with her baby from the start?

Many modern child-rearing practices are often detrimental to mother-child attachment. Separations occur at birth and continue in minor and major ways throughout development. Recent studies indicate that infants show signs of withdrawal after only one hour of separation from their mothers. Think of how many hours your baby was away from you in the hospital nursery or even in the early months of life at home. When constantly stressed by separations, a child eventually learns not to rely on his parents but to take comfort in whatever way he can. As an infant he may withdraw into himself. As an older child he may learn either to remain isolated or to be peer-oriented. If he is peer-oriented, he can become dangerously subject to negative peer pressure later on. If he is isolated, he leads a constricted life at best. We do, of course, want our children to be self-reliant. However, children whose trust in adults is strained because of too many stressful separations from the mother during infancy learn to be overly self-sufficient and refuse to allow themselves to develop any emotionally interdependent relationships. Our species would have died off if man had failed to be interdependent with others.

Children who fail to develop emotionally interdependent relationships are at higher risk for physical diseases, mental breakdown, and alcoholism as adults. When self-sufficiency is maintained at the cost of the ability to interact with other people, then it is no longer a useful quality.

The more a mother and child are together, the greater the opportunity for good attachment. If the mother has the baby on her body in a baby carrier, she learns to know the meaning of her baby's every move. Eskimo mothers have always amazed more "civilized" mothers because they know beforehand when the baby will urinate or defecate. The less a mother and baby are in touch physically, the less opportunity the mother has to learn the baby's cues and the stronger the baby's cues must be in order to communicate. For example, if the baby is in a crib in a bedroom, the mother cannot hear little noises to know the baby is awake. The baby must yell to attract the mother's attention. In contrast, a baby carried on the mother's body needs only to gurgle to tell the mother he is awake. A slight squawk tells her he is hungry. The separated baby needs to cry or scream to convey his need. It is obvious which kind of communication is more rewarding for both mother and baby. If the baby cannot be on the mother's body or at least in the same room, a good alternative is an intercom between baby's room and mother's location, so the mother can hear the cues and avoid training the child to scream for attention. In the case of an older baby or young child, a more common reaction to unmet needs is giving up or withdrawal. They often learn to cope with their unmet needs but at the expense of their trust in their mothers and thereafter in adults generally. They learn to devalue their feelings. For example, children are expected to overcome their feelings of pain, fear, and loss resulting from separation. In order to cope, they must lessen their attachment to Mother. Studies have shown that children are finally ready at age four, not earlier, to sustain separation from the mother without impairing their ability to attach. Practice does not make them ready for separation. A well-attached child who is ready to separate does not cling. An insecure child clings. Of course as a practical matter there are many unavoidable separations, but we should recognize that there is a cost, ranging from trivial to immense, depending on the extent of the separations and how they are handled. Sometimes just being aware that there are consequences helps a mother to take steps to counteract them. *Holding time* is a direct and effective way.

Attachment is fostered by a mutually gratifying interaction, both verbal and physical. If your child's needs are thwarted by your actions or omissions, then the child will behave in ways that are not gratifying to you. For example, Jeanne's mother spends less than half an hour a day in direct one-to-one contact with her. Yes, they do spend time together doing things such as going to the YWCA or to music lessons, but there is little intense and truly satisfying contact. Jeanne's behavior makes it apparent that she needs either more attention or more effective attention. She is oppositional and provocative most of the time. She snatches food she is not supposed to have right before her mother's eyes, asking to be stopped. She starts fights with her older brother. She whines constantly. The hugs her mother gives her stop the bad behavior for a few minutes. Jeanne needs *holding time.* This intense contact would satisfy Jeanne's need for attention and at the same time give her an outlet for her feelings and thus remove the need to act badly.

Some children seem to need a great deal of attention, while others are satisfied with very little. Ginny acted as though she was starving for attention no matter how much time her mother spent with her; in fact, she behaved very much like Jeanne. On the other hand, Bobby, her playmate from infancy, was easy to satisfy. He took advantage of any time his mother spent with him to make good contact. Actually, because of her very busy career, his mother spent much less time with him than Ginny's mother did with her. However, Bobby's mother had had better mothering herself, and making contact came naturally. Ginny's mother had suffered emotional deprivation at the hands of a mother who never paid much attention to her. Mothering does not come naturally. Mothering *the way you were mothered* comes naturally. *Holding time* can offset this pattern when it is detrimental and strengthen it when it is good enough. After several sessions, Ginny said to her mother one day, "Mommy, you're becoming more like Bobby's mother." Ginny's mother felt gratified because she had always been acutely aware of the differences and had felt helpless to change her pattern.

A mother and child communicate through voice, eye contact, and touch. The sense of touch is most important in early life. Extra touching can overcome irritability and even physical maturational delays, such as those found in premature babies. A study of two matched groups of newborns showed that babies in the group given extra loving care by the nurses were calm and happy. Babies in the other group cried a great deal. When the treatment was reversed, the second group became calm and happy and the first group cried. Another study showed that premature newborns caught up to their normal agemates in developmental maturation by kindergarten if they were massaged and given passive movement exercise three times a day in the first months of life.

Touch is necessary not only for the survival of all living organisms but also for the well-being of all humans. In extreme cases of touch deprivation, if the deprivation is not reversed in time, infants fail to thrive and sometimes even die.

The fact that the tactile system is the earliest to develop in humans and in all animals indicates how important it is. The skin, the largest sensing organ, houses different types of sensory receptors; these receptors, in various concentrations at different locations, tell the brain where and what type of touch is occurring. Pleasurable touch can take such forms as caressing, cuddling, hugging, stroking, or holding.

Each touch, no matter how light, conveys a variety of messages to the brain by way of electrochemical impulses. One small touch can create a great deal of brain activity. Therefore, when someone touches you, he or she has a big impact on your brain. Multiply the physical effect of one touch by all the touch impulses received from being hugged. You can understand the greatly increased response that takes place in the brain when touching extends to hugging. Not only is the response magnified many times, but also the associations that are triggered by being hugged have a profound effect on the child. First of all, the child feels the hug. Second, the hug feels good physically. Third, it takes on emotional meaning.

One evening I was with a group that included a three-month-old without her mother. No one could soothe the baby. I held her as tightly as I could, and she calmed down. If I loosened my grip, she cried. If I tightened it again, she calmed. Certainly that baby felt safe when tightly held. Earlier, she had spent a few hours crying because there had been no one there who could comfort her effectively. Her mother no doubt would have found a way.

My own baby wanted to be stroked when he was one day old. He kept putting his forearm on my fingernails and moving it up and down. At first I thought I was imagining it. But he continued to move his arm to my nails if I moved away. He was definitely asking to be stroked. He also sought a great deal of eye contact with me—more than I would have responded to if I had not known that gazing into his eyes was important for our bonding together.

Two fascinating studies show how touch is still of prime importance later in life. One experiment involved a girl asking strangers for a dime to make a phone call. If she just asked nicely, she got the dime about half the time. When she touched the people to get their attention, she got the dime from more than 90 percent. A second study showed that subliminal touch, which is a touch so slight that it is not consciously perceived, is more powerful than a friendly verbal interchange. The study involved a librarian handing back the borrower's card: one group of borrowers was pleasantly greeted by the librarian; the other group was only touched on the finger in an unnoticeable way as she handed back the card. The two groups were interviewed about their impressions of the library. The second group had a markedly more positive view than the first, despite the fact that the librarian had spoken to the untouched group in a very friendly way.

Many other studies have been done and new ones are in progress to further explore the benefits of touch. I am sure that you want to touch your child and that you enjoy physical affection from your child. However, *holding time* goes beyond touching or even hugging. You must exclude all distractions, sit down in a comfortable, safe, private place with your child, and begin an intense physical and emotional experience. You must continue this contact until both of you are feeling blissfully happy and strongly connected. We have noticed that mother and child even breathe in unison after a good session.

You may be wondering by now whether you and your child really need such an intense experience. My experience has shown that it is good for everyone. The following questions will start you thinking about ways that *holding time* would be especially helpful to you.

When you're out of the house, do you wish you could stay away longer?

Do you have to threaten or lose your temper with your children to obtain results?

Do you feel that all you do is give, give, give, with no time left for yourself?

Do your children fight or embarrass you in front of other people?

Does your child reject physical affection from you except on his terms?

If you have answered yes to some or all of these questions, then you and your family will benefit from *holding time.* The rewards a family reaps may vary according to the individuals, but there are many which seem to be universal.

The greatest benefit is the profound connection you will experience with your child. You will develop a mutually gratifying relationship, one which is closer and more satisfying than you ever imagined possible. You will feel more confident and competent as a mother than ever before. You will enjoy having a happy, responsive child. You will find that you understand your child better, anticipate his needs sooner and more completely, and realize sooner when there is a gap between you.

Siblings benefit too. *Holding time* diminishes sibling rivalry because children whose needs have been met become more altruistic. They take care of each other, share well, become more physically demonstrative with each other, and play together more. The underlying cause of sibling rivalry is a child's feeling that he is not getting enough of his mother. Once a child feels he is getting enough, he no longer feels threatened by a sibling.

After just one full cycle from confrontation through rejection to resolution, neither you nor your child will ever be afraid of sharing feelings again. Your child will be more independent without being more isolated, more affectionate, loving, and responsive without being clingy, more confident, more responsible, and more motivated to develop his potential because of the secure base that *holding time* provides.

Opening channels of deep communication allows both of you

complete freedom of expression. Your child gets in touch with his feelings, you get in touch with yours, and both of you get in touch with each other's. You both learn that you can survive each other's anger and feel closer because of it.

If you give your child a safe outlet for emotional distress, he will no longer need to show you how he feels with temper tantrums or defiance. The list of distress signals that *holding time* mitigates is a long one: sibling rivalry, clinging, shyness, sleep disturbances, bed-wetting, stealing and other antisocial behavior, stuttering and speech delays, whining, destructive or dangerous acts, and tantrums.

Furthermore, it puts the parents in charge of the child, the safest situation for a child to be in. It gives the parents a tool for handling a child's upsets or bad behavior. It gives them a way of becoming closer when they feel distant. It gives parents a way to compensate for mistakes they make, as everyone does. It gives parents a way to make up for absences and even for accidents of life that divert attention, such as a family member's illness or death or other life crisis. It makes parents feel more confident in their parenting, knowing they are doing everything they can for their children. It gives them a better way to deal with the normal upheavals of child development and of life itself.

Even very small children can learn to channel their upsets. Danny, age two and a half, whose mother had been using *holding time* for several months, one day began to cry bitterly the minute she picked him up for his regular afternoon session of close contact. The mother assumed she had scratched him. "No," he said, "Wendy hurt my feelings this morning." The mother was surprised that little Danny had waited all day to tell her of this injury. Thanks to their contact, she was spared an incident in the morning between Wendy and Danny. Her child was spared an unresolved upset because he was able to share his feelings with his mom. Furthermore, his self-esteem was enhanced by his successful self-control.

Emily doesn't want to hold.

She cries.

She pulls her mother's hair.

She refuses contact by shutting her eyes.

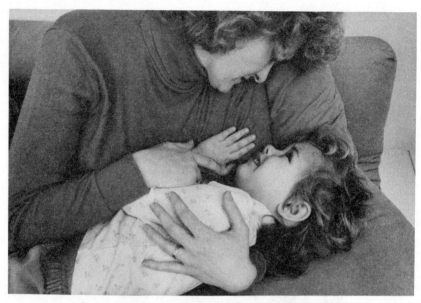

After a protracted struggle, Emily allows eye contact.

She begins to relax into close contact.

They both begin to feel better.

She offers her mother a kiss.

39

They begin to talk.

Emily shares her secret feelings.

She stays with Mom despite distractions.

They achieve deep communication and contact.

The close communication during *holding time* informs the mother of the reason behind a child's misbehavior so that instead of punishing the bad behavior, which often only alienates mother and child further, the mother can directly address the feelings and the cause of the upset. For example, one day when my own son was seven, he was being obnoxious, which puzzled me because he is generally well behaved. When I next held him, he told me that he was very upset because I had just concluded negotiations on writing this book. He thought it meant that I would have no time for playing with him on our vacation. He was relieved to learn that I would still pay attention to him, and I was relieved to learn why he was behaving so provocatively.

Holding time helps you deal with conflict from areas that have become battlegrounds, such as bedtime, eating, toothbrushing, chores, or homework. Because the mother and child are in good communication and have a way of dealing with their anger, upset feelings no longer result in bad behavior. Instead, upsets are resolved. When a new battleground does start to develop, dealing with it immediately and in an effective way gets rid of anger and brings mother and child closer together. For the child's part, he does not just see his mother's angry responses but comes to understand his mother's fear, concern, and reason for an action or inaction. When he understands her feelings and reasons, he becomes more responsive to her wishes.

Holding time helps the mother to set limits; she no longer reacts by setting unreasonable ones out of anger or frustration, because these feelings are worked out. It also helps her to avoid feeling guilty about saying no and about setting limits when it is important to do so. A child feels much better and is more secure having definite limits. One child told her baby-sitter, "I want Mommy to tell me to stop wetting my pants."

The close connection increases your ability to focus your attention on your child when you have time to play together. You will not need a third person, TV, or playground for diversion. You will really enjoy one-to-one interaction. Your child will be able to transfer this good way of relating with you to other people in and outside of the family. This ability to form strong positive relationships is especially useful if you leave your child with a care-giver. If your child's relationship with the care-giver is mutually satisfying, you will be more likely to keep the same person for a long time, which has many benefits to you and especially to your child. In addition, your child will be learning good parenting.

Three-year-old Emily, pictured in this chapter, demonstrates how early children learn parenting. At a restaurant with her baby-sitter she heard a mother in the next booth threatening to slap her two children if they didn't stop misbehaving. "Excuse me, lady," she said, "but we don't slap. We talk and cuddle and sometimes do holding." When the surprised woman asked Emily what happens when she misbehaves, she answered, "Mom and I hold and get our angries out." In addition to having the self-confidence to speak out, Emily had already formed a concept of effective parenting and a value for treating people with compassionate understanding.

Holding time helps mother and children cope with separations by helping them to connect before and after and to understand each other's feelings about the separations. If the mother is working, it helps give her a good enough connection with her child to feel less divided when she is involved in work or career pursuits.

Holding time's benefits for each stage of development will be discussed in Part II. But first let's consider specifically what it is and how it works.

3.

HOW DOES IT WORK?

How Do I Do It?

Everyone agrees that hugging is good for children—
and for mothers too, for that matter. How often have you heard
a mother plead, "Come on, give me a hug," when the child is
reluctant?

Hugging depends on both mother and child's simultaneous
willingness to come together. Hugging can be finished in a few
seconds. It feels good and conveys a message of caring and
giving. Of course, hugging can extend into holding. Such holding is usually a mutually agreed-upon and pleasant interaction
in which both you and your child put your arms around each
other and snuggle into each other's bodies. Or holding can be
initiated by you alone with you as the giver and your child as
the recipient. This latter holding mode can evolve into what I
call *holding time.*

In *holding time,* you physically embrace your child whether
or not either of you feels, at that moment, the usual emotions

that lead to an embrace. It does not necessarily begin with—but should never end without reaching—a happy phase of closeness. *Holding time* uses intense physical and emotional contact to reinforce the connection between you and your child. The better the connection, the more understanding you will have of each other. The better the understanding, the more open you will be to each other's feelings. With no barriers between you, a closer and more satisfying relationship will be possible. One mother who changed her lifestyle to make room for this method with each of her three children, as well as with her husband and her mother, said, "Holding has established a bond in our family that has transcended every problem."

Unless you have an open channel of easy communication coupled with a mutually demonstrative physical closeness, a child will feel deprived. Sometimes a mother will also feel deprived, especially if she had this type of close relationship with another of her children or with her parents when she was a child. If one of them feels deprived, resentment and anger build up. These negative feelings are acted out in small ways, for example through the child's annoying demands and constant whining and the mother's nagging, or vice versa. The open communication and physical closeness that result from *holding time* preclude those behaviors because anger and resentment are worked out during each session. Just the act of communicating is in itself supportive and comforting. Beyond that, you and your child learn to convey your needs in a way that elicits a positive response from each other.

Lacking such an exchange, a child learns to repress or deny his true feelings. Say your child has been told not to hit, not to throw things, to stop yelling or teasing. His conclusion might be that he must hide or store his anger, since he has not mastered any effective and acceptable way of expressing it. Alternatively he may release it in other, more destructive ways. Because his feelings seem unacceptable, he develops low self-esteem. As he grows up, his positive development is thwarted by this low self-esteem, and his repressed anger and resentment will be acted out in unacceptable behavior.

Holding conveys a message to your child that you genuinely accept him and his full range of feelings, no matter how negative or destructive the feelings may be. The advantage is that these emotions are allowed expression primarily during the holding experience and therefore need not be released through bad behavior. Instead they are ventilated, discussed, experienced, and shared. The fact that the mother asks for the expression of the full range of emotions gives a child permission to experience them without guilt or shame. Because his mother can tolerate the expression of all his feelings, there is no need for the child to devalue himself. The child learns that feelings need not frighten him. Every feeling can be processed in this setting— fear, anger, guilt, shame, hurt, envy, jealousy, and all positive feelings as well.

How many people can *easily* say "I love you" to their parents, their children, or even their spouses? We have impaired our ability to express our positive feelings by impairing our ability to express the negative ones. When one set of emotions is blocked, the other set is inhibited. In order to keep the lid on the bad feelings, people tend to keep the lid on the good.

Now let's take the lid off and see how *holding time* works. It usually has three phases: confrontation, rejection, and resolution.

Confrontation is a brief phase during which you and your child come together to initiate *holding.* It begins when you take your child on your lap. It may begin as a quiet time of comfort and closeness. If, on the other hand, this is an unplanned session that you initiate because of misbehavior or a tantrum, then it may progress quickly, even instantaneously, to the rejection phase. In the first stage, you and your child are each tuned in to your own thoughts and feelings. As you each move on to try to be in touch with the other, you both begin to feel the hurt and anger provoked either by the barriers you experience or by specific clashes you have had in the previous hours or days. The child may also express hurt or anger over actions by friends, siblings, or teachers. It is even useful for you to sometimes express your own anger arising from outside sources so that your child isn't burdened by the belief that he is always the cause when you are angry or upset. *Holding time* allows both of you to discharge your pent-up agression in a safe way.

As you continue to hold, confrontation will either gradually or suddenly lead to rejection, the second stage of *holding time.* Your child will begin to resist you. He may fight you physically, verbally, or both. As you hold on despite the child's entreaties to let him go, his full range of feelings will begin to emerge, usually starting with anger but sometimes with fear or sadness. There follow one or more cycles of anguished outbursts alternating with quieter moments during which the child may be calmer and rejection seems to wane. A successful *holding* will not be complete, however, until the calm period achieves true resolution, the final phase.

Resolution is marked by a sweet molding together of the mother and child, physically and emotionally. The pair relax in each other's arms, gaze into each other's eyes, and offer tender physical caresses. They feel a closeness that goes beyond mere cuddling or hugging. However long this stage may last, mother and child both seem to wish it would go on indefinitely. Neither rushes to stop it. Ultimately the session ends as mother and child return to their routine activities but now with relief, joy, and greater mutual understanding. If mother and child play afterward, the play is different from the usual pattern. The child is brimming over with enthusiasm and enjoyment and a wish to share his pleasure with his mother. Even mothers who normally don't enjoy playing with their children describe great satisfaction with this activity just after a resolution.

Now you have a brief outline of a holding session. Next we will move on to an in-depth discussion of what to expect when you start a program with your child. A few other general points should be made at this juncture.

First, there is no standard session. Like many human endeavors, it is by nature quite variable. This is a function of multiple factors, including the moods of the participants; the issues involved, such as separation, anger, or fear; the reasons for initiating the session, be it a prearranged schedule or negative behavior that necessitates a spontaneous confrontation; the period since the last *holding;* the presence or absence of the father, siblings, or grandparents; the plan or absence of a plan for the day's activities; the mother's work outside the home; the day of the week; the fatigue level of child or mother—the list could go on.

The length of the sessions will vary also, depending on many of these factors, especially the issues to be resolved, the ease of achieving resolution, and the willingness of the mother to release her own emotions. As with most activities, practice will influence its duration and outcome. Initial sessions may be quite different from those after substantial experience. As you and your child develop individually and as a mutually interdependent pair, your experience will change. With practice you may be able sometimes to reach a resolution in a few minutes.

It is important to remember that you and your child are unique individuals who will find your own most appropriate style. Problems that confront you may be different from those of other mother-child pairs and different with you from child to child. Nevertheless, there is also a happy uniformity to *holding time,* and I hope the following discussion will anticipate your concerns, answer any questions, relieve your doubts, and open up to you the benefits that this technique offers in the hands of caring parents.

The three phases tend to have a continuous flow, one into the next, but you may find that you go back and forth between rejection and resolution as one issue is resolved and then a new one is addressed. Let's explore these phases a little further.

I. CONFRONTATION

Choose a time when you can devote at least an hour to your first session. Find a private, quiet, comfortable place. Ideally the spot you choose should be far enough from other people so that you will not have to be concerned about making noise. If anyone does ask you later what the racket was about, tell them that you and your child were practicing expressing anger in a safe and harmless, though sometimes noisy, way. Once reassured, people are usually understanding and often very interested in such a process. Holders who live in apartments often explain to their neighbors, even before they are asked, that they are practicing *holding time.* Children have told me how much it meant to them that their mothers put them ahead of worries about what people would think if they overheard a particularly noisy session.

Once you have decided on a spot, eliminate all possible distractions: put on some comfortable clothes; go to the bathroom; take the phone off the hook. Once your child has gone to the bathroom too, ask him to join you in your chosen spot. Put your child on your lap with his legs around your waist and his arms tucked under your armpits. Explain to him that you want to spend some time being very close in order to share feelings. If you find this position difficult, an alternative is to hold the child across your lap as you would hold a baby for cuddling or breast feeding. This gives the right distance for eye contact and some mothers find it easier to maintain. For much older children, sitting side by side on a couch or lying down on a bed works best.

A holding session evolves differently depending upon the circumstances leading to it and upon the individuals involved. Some children begin to cuddle at this point. Enjoy it. But don't let go! As you hold on, the child will begin to squirm and fuss or argue about getting down.

Amy, a three-year-old who began *holding time* at fifteen months, asks to do it daily. Nevertheless she always objects to the immediate prospect even before she reaches what she calls the "holding chair." If her mother says it's time, she offers excuses, such as, "You promised I could watch TV," "I'm hungry," "I have to go to the bathroom," "I don't have any angries," "My angries flew away." So, for Amy, confrontation leads to rejection as soon as her mother insists that it really is time and holds on so Amy can't escape.

On the rare occasions when Amy does not express her feelings soon after the start, her mother searches for subjects of distress: "Are you angry that I had to go to work today?" "Why can't you cooperate when we have to leave the playground?" "It makes me angry when you run away every time I try to help you dress to go out!" "That makes me yell, and I don't want to yell at you." Something will eventually strike a chord, and the child will respond by turning away, fighting, telling her mother not to say that, or indicating in some other way that it is a sensitive subject. Thus the next phase, rejection, will begin.

Perhaps instead your child may be comfortable in your arms, not responding to your attempts to arouse his feelings but at the same time keeping his attention elsewhere. He may look out the window and try to direct the subject to the trees or clouds, or he may focus on something in the room. Your insistence that he look at you, even by physically forcing him to look at you, will bring on the resistance that will lead to rejection.

Finally, if your child does not express any upset while you continue to hold, you can usually elicit his feelings by expressing your own anger or frustration or demands or wishes with increasing forcefulness. Never has any child failed to respond when the mother has finally reached the depths of her own despair over not reaching her child. If the mother holds back, the child will often hold back. But if the mother expresses her deepest feelings in an appropriately emotional way, for example with tears, then the child invariably responds.

II. *REJECTION*

Rejection begins as the child tries to escape your embrace, your gaze, or your words. The child may spit, kick, writhe, butt, scream, turn purple with rage—or his sad crying may break your heart. But if you hold on until his distress ends, you will reach a kind of communication that you didn't know was possible. The excuses a child will concoct to convince you to let go may be quite imaginative. He may suddenly decide he needs to do a chore he usually resists: "I have to go clean up my room." Even a young child will sometimes question the fairness of using this type of force. However, holding on will lead you to conclude that he is testing you, gauging your determination and your willingness to hear whatever is inside him no matter how scary or terrible it seems to him. He may say provocative things, such as, "I don't love you," "I don't want you," "I love Daddy, not you." You can respond with "It hurts my feelings when you say that" or "I love you very much, and I need your love too." Your willingness to share your pain in the face of your child's rejection will eventually elicit the sympathy and caring that is the beginning of the two-way street you are trying to establish.

Sometimes the child may only be able to express the raw emotions of his anger or sadness with screams or mournful crying. It is important to let this happen, even though it is painful to watch.

When we first used this technique with normal children, we were very puzzled by the extent of the fight they gave their mothers time after time. I asked some of them why they put up such a fight if they really did want to be held. One child said, "It helps me get angries out." An older child said, "It makes me feel good to know that whatever happens, I can take my upset to my mom in holding." We learned that even the two- and three-year-olds saved their upsets for *holding time.*

When his anger is at its height, your child will most likely avoid looking into your eyes. This may even be the focus of the battle. You can ask, "Why can't you look at me? What did I do that made you so angry that you can't even look at me?" When the struggle stops and you are gazing lovingly into each other's eyes, then you know you have finished this phase, whether you have all the answers or not.

You increase your chance of achieving a good resolution if both of you have expressed your full range of feelings: hurt, anger, fear. If, while holding fast, you have told your child how his actions make you feel, then you have conveyed the message, "Nothing can come between us—not your anger and not even my anger."

You can see that this interaction involves both you and your child equally. It is not just some action you thrust upon him. It is an attempt to establish yourself as the loving mediator of his feelings and experiences. But you can be helpful only if your child is free to bring those feelings and experiences to you. Often your child tells you things in ways so small compared to whatever else is going on around you that you don't catch the message. *Holding* can help you keep from missing the clues.

Eventually you will also want your child to tell you the source of these emotions. You can ask why he is so sad or angry. If he cannot or will not begin to tell you, you can propose possibilities, such as, "Are you angry that I talked so long on the phone?" "That I yelled at you?" "That I had to work today?" You will learn to see signs, such as heightened crying or more forceful struggle to escape, that you are nearing the mark. This method of fishing may especially help a younger child to learn what the possible answers are.

Mothers sometimes worry about putting ideas into their children's heads. This concern is not supported by my experience. If the mother's suggestion does not match the child's thoughts and feelings, he will discard it. But if the child denies it vehemently, you may have hit the mark. In any case, you will not be putting ideas into his head.

Mothers who are new to this method may be frustrated by

feeling that their child cannot express the source of his rage. Eventually they will be amazed by the ease with which even very young children can express the source once they become experienced holders. In time and with practice, your child will learn to verbalize effectively.

For example, when Becky was three she began throwing things at her parents; this behavior continued for two weeks. It was unusual because she had been doing *holding* fairly regularly for over a year, and such outbursts were rare and never persisted. Finally, during their session, she told her mother, "I throw things because you left me with Helen." Helen was the one-day substitute for her beloved baby-sitter, who had taken a sick day two weeks earlier. The parents were surprised at this direct answer and relieved to know the cause of this sudden throwing behavior. The throwing stopped after that session.

I had not guessed the extent to which a young child could get in touch with feelings *and* put them into words in a rather sophisticated way, certainly beyond what would seem usual for the age level. Over time, I came to the conclusion that children are capable of much more verbalization than they have been given credit for and that we must be keeping children from being in touch with their feelings by not being in touch ourselves either with our own feelings or with theirs. After using *holding time* for two years, one mother wrote, "I feel good about my mothering, knowing I have done everything I can. My child feels good because she experiences my love and sees how much I am risking by getting in touch with my deepest feelings of rejection. The benefit to both of us is the enjoyment we feel being with one another . . . I would say that holding is the tool that is sculpting two beautiful lives out of a former mixture of upset, confusion, denial, anger, and frustration."

As you can see, the most important part of the rejection phase is for mother and child to communicate their deepest feelings of distress to each other. *The mother must act as a role model* by freeing up her feelings. This is often hard to do; it sometimes requires practice. Some mothers have suppressed their emotions so much that they feel they have to playact at first. But if they resolve to try, they usually succeed. Motivation is the most important factor in success of any kind, and this is no exception.

III. *RESOLUTION*

When both mother and child have reached to the depths of their feelings, a catharsis occurs and the resolution begins. The struggling, fighting, screaming, and avoidance behavior of rejection give way to an intense closeness—both physical and verbal. The child usually begins to caress the mother's face and to melt into her body. His gaze is direct and tender. The decidedly hurtful comments expressed during rejection are replaced by statements of love and affection: "Momma, you are beautiful," "I love you," and so forth.

If you have released your own pent-up emotions, your child may console you by wiping your tears or by other shared intimacies. He may say, "You don't have to worry anymore," or, "Did you get your angries out?"

With resolution comes a complete change from the intense struggle that went on before. It is surprising how loving and tender a child can be, even though minutes before he was fighting, screaming, and trying every device to turn you away. Finally, when he knows you have accepted everything that was stored up inside him, the flood of relief in his face is truly wonderful. The feelings of closeness, safety, relief, and joy surround you. Your child, who may be too busy at other times for more than a quick hug, lingers in your embrace willingly, gazing straight into your eyes.

For mothers the resolution is a most rewarding time. They often liken this closeness to the time when they were breastfeeding their babies or cuddling them to sleep. Some mothers sadly say that their children let themselves be held like this only in the first three years of life. If you feel this way, you can change this pattern right now, no matter how old your child is. It is not too late to start *holding time.* You owe it to your child and you owe it to yourself.

Sometimes only a partial resolution is reached. Many of the pent-up feelings may have been released, but other sources of distress may not have been dealt with. If you have the time and energy, you should keep holding until it is all out. You can sense that there is still some unexpressed emotion if your child is relieved and yet anxious to bound off your lap to go on to other things. After a really complete resolution, you both feel like holding on to the blissful comfort indefinitely. If you have not achieved this, holding on longer will lead to a new confrontation, rejection, and resolution.

Under some circumstances, a partial resolution may fit your needs. If you initiated the session because of a specific fear (such as thunder and lightning) or inappropriate behavior (running into the street, throwing a toy, hitting a sibling), then dealing with the feelings and concerns you both have about that one issue may be all you want. A partial resolution will have some of the features mentioned above but perhaps not all. If you get only a partial resolution, the next time you will try for a more complete one.

On occasion your child may fall asleep. This is especially likely if some of the distress he had felt beforehand had been preventing him from relaxing enough to nap or sleep properly. He may finally surrender to accumulated exhaustion. This may or may not constitute a complete resolution. When the child awakes, the characteristics of a complete resolution described above, such as affection, contentment, and a desire to remain physically close, should be present. If not, a new rejection phase may follow and the cycle may resume until you reach a complete resolution. Sometimes both of you may be too tired to continue. If this is the case, you can return in a subsequent session to the issues you had addressed. Even if you do not reach a good resolution, you will experience some degree of increased communication, closeness, and cooperation.

As I stated earlier, different holding sessions will be of different duration. They may vary from day to day depending on events of the day or week, issues to be worked out, and the ability of mother and child to unleash their emotions. Your initial session is apt to be one of the longest, since you will both be new to the experience. Whatever the duration, it is best to continue, when able, to a complete resolution each time so as to obtain the fullest possible benefits.

If you and your child do not work through the anger during *holding,* it is possible that you may even feel worse at first. Or your child may feel better but you may feel worse, even though you see by his behavior that he is improved. Often the two of you have been maintaining a delicate balance, and each has kept a certain distance in order to preserve it. However, this precarious balance is not constructive over the long term, because your child or both of you may be accumulating a reservoir of anger and hurt that eventually will disturb it anyway. *Holding time* might at first disrupt that tacit arrangement. Don't worry. You will most definitely arrive at a better balance as you practice it. The more resolve you have to hold on until you both feel better, the sooner you will reach this happy result. The newfound security derived from open communication and physical closeness will offset any imagined or real negative consequences while you are on-your way to that goal.

Mothers often worry about destroying what they feel is an already tenuous connection with their children. Such worries sometimes stem from guilt feelings caused by not spending enough time together, or from the mother's feelings of inadequacy in handling them, or from the mother's slightly negative feelings toward the children, especially when there is a great deal of sibling rivalry or when the father appears to have a better relationship with them. If you have such a worry, then *holding time* will be especially helpful to you.

Now you may be asking yourself, "Do I dare hold my child against his will?" Judge by the result. When children experience the closeness as well as the emotional release after a resolution, they usually show by their feelings and actions how much they have benefited. They become more affectionate, more cooperative, and calmer. Many children then begin to ask for *holding.* Others continue to protest but provoke you or remind you about it indirectly through misbehavior or teasing until you do it again.

Whether your child protests or not, you will find that doing it strengthens your ties. The most important gift you can give your child is a strong, loving, enduring bond with you. Such a bond gives your child a safe base from which to explore the outside world and his relationships with other people, as well as his own inner feelings, thoughts, capabilities, and interests. The stronger your connection, the freer he is to reach out to others and to succeed in the world. If you are worried, that means your connection needs strengthening.

If you are not worried, you will feel free to do *holding time,* knowing that you can only improve things for yourself and your child by becoming closer and by offering yourself as a receptacle for his unprocessed or pent-up feelings. Best of all, you can easily find out for yourself how it will benefit you and your child by trying it.

Before you begin, please fill out this checklist. Then put it aside. At the end of the book, after you have practiced *holding time,* you will be asked to fill it out again. You will find your scores dramatically different. This checklist and its second part will act as a guide to your progress. You may wish to complete it after reading the book, again after one session, after a few weeks, and from time to time thereafter.

PART ONE: THE "WHO NEEDS HOLDING TIME?" CHECKLIST

SCORE:	1	2	3
1. When you are out of the house, do you wish you could stay away longer?	OFTEN ___	SOMETIMES ___	NEVER ___
2. When your child is difficult, do you wish someone else would take over the situation?	OFTEN ___	SOMETIMES ___	NEVER ___
3. Do you feel jealous when your child seems to prefer someone else to you?	OFTEN ___	SOMETIMES ___	NEVER ___
4. Do you find one of your children easier to deal with than another?	OFTEN ___	SOMETIMES ___	NEVER ___
5. Do you feel closer to one child than to another?	OFTEN ___	SOMETIMES ___	NEVER ___
6. Do you envy another mother's relationship with her child?	OFTEN ___	SOMETIMES ___	NEVER ___
7. Do you feel you are a better mother to one of your children than to another?	OFTEN ___	SOMETIMES ___	NEVER ___
8. Do you feel some mothers are better than you?	OFTEN ___	SOMETIMES ___	NEVER ___
9. Do you lose your temper with your child?	OFTEN ___	SOMETIMES ___	NEVER ___

10. Do you have to ask your child more than once to do things?   OFTEN ___ SOMETIMES ___ NEVER ___

11. Do you have to ask your child more than once to stop doing something?   OFTEN ___ SOMETIMES ___ NEVER ___

12. Do you have to threaten in order to obtain results?   OFTEN ___ SOMETIMES ___ NEVER ___

13. Do you feel that you have no time for yourself?   OFTEN ___ SOMETIMES ___ NEVER ___

14. Do you feel that all you do is give, give, give?   OFTEN ___ SOMETIMES ___ NEVER ___

15. Do your children fight?   OFTEN ___ SOMETIMES ___ NEVER ___

16. Does your child have problems with peers?   OFTEN ___ SOMETIMES ___ NEVER ___

17. Does your child cling to you?   OFTEN ___ SOMETIMES ___ NEVER ___

18. Is your child extremely independent for his/her age?   OFTEN ___ SOMETIMES ___ NEVER ___

19. Does your husband disagree with your handling of your child?   OFTEN ___ SOMETIMES ___ NEVER ___

20. Does your husband contradict you with the child?   OFTEN ___ SOMETIMES ___ NEVER ___

21. Are you annoyed with your husband for not doing his share of child care?   OFTEN ___ SOMETIMES ___ NEVER ___

SCORE:	1	2	3
22. Are you embarrassed by your child's behavior in front of your friends or strangers?	OFTEN ___	SOMETIMES ___	NEVER ___
23. Does your child have difficulty adjusting to change?	OFTEN ___	SOMETIMES ___	NEVER ___
24. Is your child defiant?	OFTEN ___	SOMETIMES ___	NEVER ___
25. Does your child dawdle?	OFTEN ___	SOMETIMES ___	NEVER ___
26. Do you have trouble teaching your child to cooperate with household chores?	OFTEN ___	SOMETIMES ___	NEVER ___
TOTALS:	—	—	—
PART ONE TOTAL:	_____		

The following are descriptions of three mothers' experiences. All three sessions occurred just as described. They are offered as good models of what any mother might say during *holding*. However, no two sessions are alike even between the same mother and child, and your scenario may be radically different.

EXAMPLE 1

Lisa is a darling, happy, affectionate two-year-old who has a close relationship with both of her parents. Her only problem centers around her six-month-old baby brother, Danny, of whom she is very jealous. She often says to her mother that she would like to give Danny away. She grabs toys away from him and occasionally pokes him roughly. If her parents try to stop her, she has a tantrum. During one of the tantrums, Lisa's mother, Josie, decides to use *holding* for the first time.

Lisa is lying on the floor kicking and screaming. Josie picks her up, pins Lisa's legs between her own and Lisa's arms under her armpits. Josie says, "I know you are angry because Danny takes your toys and takes my attention." Lisa continues to scream and tries to pull away; Josie struggles to keep Lisa close to her in a firm embrace. The closer they become, the more Lisa tries to escape. Lisa's tantrum does not abate and the struggle intensifies.

After forty-five minutes, Josie begins to wonder if it will ever end. She decides to ease her hold and Lisa starts to calm down. But when Josie tries to talk to her, the tantrum begins all over again. Josie feels desperate and begins to cry softly. While strengthening her hold once again, she tells Lisa, "I feel so upset when you scream and fight. I can't understand why you won't let me comfort you. Please, Lisa, look at me." Lisa looks, but looking seems to make her scream even more. Josie's crying intensifies. Lisa looks at her mother and seems surprised. Josie says, "I love you, Lisa. I love Danny too. But you are my special girl. You will always be my special girl."

Though Lisa begins to calm down, she still will not look at her mother. Josie continues to cry and talk. "I get so upset when you grab toys from Danny. I know they are your toys, but Danny is just a baby. I know that he takes a lot of care and attention. I know it is hard for you to wait while I take care of him. I will try to pay more attention to you. You are my baby too." Lisa looks her mother in the eyes. Josie says, "I feel so much better when you look at me. I love you so much. You will always be my baby."

Lisa makes a little gurgling noise and shows a contented look on her face. She begins to snuggle against her mother's chest. Josie continues to explain. "Lisa, you love me and you love Daddy. You have enough love for both of us. Well, I love you and I love Daddy and I love Danny too. I have enough love for all of you." Lisa perks up. She says, "I love Granny." Josie says, "Yes, I love Granny too. We both have enough love to go around, don't we? You love Granny, you love Daddy, you love me. I love you, I love Granny, I love Daddy. And I also love little Danny. But I see I need to take better care of you. I feel better now. I hope you feel better too. I love you, Lisa. Do you have kisses for me?" Lisa kisses her mother and they cuddle. Josie says, "The next time you feel angry, let's hold." Lisa snuggles closer to her mother with a very contented look. For the rest of the day Lisa seems very peaceful and happy. She plays nicely with Danny, frequently giving her toys to him.

EXAMPLE 2

Carrie is an adorable, very verbal three-year-old. She has learned to cope with a great deal of separation from her busy mother by trying to control everyone around her. Her mother, Linda, decided to do *holding time* to help compensate for the constant separations.

No sooner has Linda picked up Carrie than the child starts snuggling comfortably. Linda says, "Carrie, I know it's hard for you when I leave every day." Carrie begins to cry and turn her head away. Linda tries to turn Carrie's face toward hers, but Carrie shuts her eyes tightly. Linda says, "Carrie, open your eyes. Please look at me. Don't pull away. I want to hold you and look at you. Carrie, please open your eyes." Linda puts her face next to Carrie's, but Carrie's efforts to avoid contact increase. She arches her back, throws back her head, and closes her eyes even more tightly. She pushes her mother with her hands and begins to cry mournfully.

Linda feels devastated by this rejection and pleads with Carrie to look at her. Carrie cries, "Let me out of here." Linda answers, "I am going to hold you until we both feel better." Carrie says, "I feel fine. Let go of me." Linda says, "I know you are angry at me, but I still love you." Carrie is unyielding. They go on struggling for forty-five minutes. Linda, devastated, sobs out loud. Carrie peeks at her. Her chubby hand reaches around her mother's back. Linda says, "Carrie, it feels good when you hold me." Carrie looks directly at her mother. Linda says, "Oh, Carrie, I love it when you look in my eyes." They both stop crying, and Carrie begins to relax and mold to her mother's body. She touches Linda's face. They cuddle for several minutes and look into each other's eyes.

EXAMPLE 3

Seven-year-old Billy is a generally well-behaved, happy, and loving child with no identifiable problems. However, his mother has a difficult time trying to balance a career and home life. She needs 100 percent cooperation from Billy when her schedule is tight. Sometimes Billy feels frustrated and somewhat oppositional. A dialogue during one of these moments goes like this:

MOTHER (*taking Billy on her lap*): "Billy, I have worked hard all day in order to be able to take you to the country this afternoon. You did not get ready when I asked you to."

BILLY: "I don't want to change my clothes."

MOTHER: "It makes me angry when I rush around to finish my work while you are in school so we can be together, and then you don't cooperate."

BILLY (*crying and struggling in his mother's tight embrace*): "I'm sorry, Mommy."

MOTHER: "I know you are, but I want you to do what I ask of you. I get frazzled when you don't do what I ask."

BILLY (*crying and struggling*): "I hate changing my clothes."

MOTHER: "I explained to you that you need the clothes in the country for school Monday."

BILLY: "I thought you could pack them."

MOTHER: "You didn't ask me. But I wasn't packing any bags anyway."

BILLY: "I didn't know that."

MOTHER: "When you don't cooperate, I feel unappreciated. I build my whole schedule around you. I need you to be pleasant to me."

BILLY: "I will, I promise. Now can we stop holding?"

MOTHER: "No, I want you to hold me too."

BILLY: "I hate holding. You're making my back hurt."

MOTHER: "If you don't pull away from me, you won't hurt your back. Put your arms around my back."

BILLY: "No, let me put my arms around your neck. Let's just hug."

MOTHER: "No, this is *holding time.* I want you to hold me and look at me."

Billy cries and struggles some more.

MOTHER: "It hurts my feelings when you refuse to hold me and look at me."

Billy still refuses. His mother starts to feel rejected and cries.

MOTHER: "Please, please look at me."

They struggle more as the mother cries. Billy feels his mother's sadness and looks at her.

MOTHER: "I love it when you look into my eyes. You used to look at me just like that when you were a tiny baby. I was so happy when you were born."

BILLY: "Don't cry, Mom."

MOTHER: "I love you, Billy."

BILLY: "I love you too."

Now Billy begins really to hold his mother tightly, and his body begins to mold to hers. He gazes into her eyes and smiles. They kiss.

MOTHER: "I love it when we hold like this."

BILLY: "Can we do this every day?"

MOTHER: "Why do you always fight me, if you want to do it every day?"

BILLY: "I only like it after."

MOTHER: "How do you feel after *holding time?*"

BILLY: "I feel as though I've never been angry and I never will be."

Billy and his mother go on cuddling. He makes no attempt to get off her lap. They continue talking. Eventually Billy asks his mother to play blocks. Both are happy as they play. Billy remains especially cooperative the rest of the day. There is an easy closeness between them.

These are examples of very good sessions with complete resolutions. Many mothers report a happy aftermath even when they can't reach a satisfying resolution. Some mothers have described doing *holding* during a tantrum in which the child finally stopped fighting but never really gave in to a cuddling phase. The negative resistance diminished but a positive coming together did not follow. Mother and child finally stopped holding and went on to other activities. The mothers said that although they felt terrible, the children seemed fine. They were calm, cheerful, quite cooperative, even enthusiastic about the next activity. One mother said, "A little lousy *holding* goes a long way." So if you don't reach a good resolution every time, wait to see what happens afterward. You may be pleasantly surprised with the positive results of the less-than-ideal *holding time.*

It is important to understand why things work. There are interesting findings from physiology that may help explain why the struggle of *holding time* could be beneficial to a child or to a mother.

We can begin with what is known about the physiology of anger. When a person is angry, adrenaline and its cousin, noradrenaline, are released. These are "fight and flight" hormones, which have helped humans and other animals survive danger since the world began. With the release of these hormones, blood pressure rises, muscle tension increases, heart rate changes, and respiratory rate increases. These reactions constitute the physical state called arousal. But arousal is the basis of many feelings, not just anger. Anger shares the physiological symptoms of many emotions: joy, excitement, fear, anxiety, frustration, and jealousy. Other causes of increased adrenaline include noise, heat, exercise, hunger, and crowds. People interpret their emotional response to arousal according to their perception of the cause. For example, many runners revel in the arousal of exercise. However, an equal degree of arousal caused by noise or frustration might feel very unpleasant to that same person. A runner who is aroused by anger can, by running, transform the anger into the arousal of exercise. Afterward he might transform the arousal of exercise into the arousal of excitement through another activity, such as creative work or sex. The duration and intensity of arousal and the relaxation afterward can be very pleasurable. But another person might feel only exhausted, especially if he had learned to view arousal as unpleasant. In fact, he might spend a great deal of effort to avoid arousal altogether.

It is almost self-evident that our perceptions are colored by emotions and, conversely, that our emotions are affected by our perceptions. An ingenious cat-and-mouse study illustrates that perceptions can also be modified by other perceptions. A cat's auditory response to a ticking metronome was recorded by electrodes in the part of the brain that registers sounds. But when a mouse was placed next to the ticking metronome, the ticking no longer registered in the cat's brain—the electrodes received no signal! The cat's perception of the mouse obliterated the perception of the ticking. Imagine how many perceptions are distorted or missed entirely by a child whose life has been dominated by anxiety, frustration, fear, anger, or jealousy because his basic needs have not been met during his early life. It would be harder to convince that child that arousal is pleasurable than it would be to convince a child whose arousal had come mainly from positive sources. The child who experiences arousal as painful or as a sign of danger will work harder to block all arousal, because the block is serving to protect him from painful feelings. However, the block often overreaches, protecting him from good feelings as well. The object is to release that block.

I suggest that noradrenaline and adrenaline begin to flow during the physical struggle of *holding time,* the way they would in any exercise as part of the cardiovascular response to muscular exertion. The arousal of the physical struggle usually gives way to the arousal of anger when the mother intensifies her efforts to maintain her hold on the child against his will. As the struggle continues, the child usually experiences a whole range of emotions, but in the safety of his mother's arms. This time the state of arousal is associated with being held lovingly, resolutely, and closely. (In fact, children have told me that they feel very grateful and relieved to be able to express angry feelings without being rejected by their mothers.) If the child feels this safety as his mother persists, arousal of emotions reaches a crescendo. After the peak, the arousal is usually transformed to joy and pleasure as the two begin an affectionate embrace. The state of arousal gradually diminishes as mother and child relax in each other's arms.

The neurobiology of attachment suggests that two sets of brain chemicals balance each other to produce the right amount of arousal in a young child. The hormone of arousal, noradrenaline, causes a decrease in clinging behavior, which in turn leads to play and exploration. The other set of brain chemicals, called endogenous opioids, which have been found to decrease feelings of separation anxiety, are released when the child makes comforting physical contact with the mother. It is thought that young children alternately stimulate these two systems by going back and forth between exploration and physical contact.

A child can remain in a constant state of hyperarousal if his mother is not adequately responsive to his attempts to alternate appropriately between clinging and play or exploration. A constant state of hyperarousal is believed to have detrimental long-term effects on the ability to regulate strong emotions. I believe that *holding time* helps a mother and child to maintain the right amount of arousal and therefore to regulate strong emotions.

I suggest that the physical struggle elicits adrenaline and noradrenaline during the rejection phase, while the endogenous opioids are released during the resolution. The children seesaw back and forth several times between rejection and resolution in a way that mimics the seesawing back and forth between clinging and exploration observed in primate young. The alternation of noradrenaline and the opioids and the way it seems to correlate with the rejection and resolution phases could certainly explain what happens during the *holding time* sequence and what follows. After a complete resolution, the children cling in a way that is most satisfying to both mother and child. This clinging or cuddling phase can last as long as thirty minutes. The children appear to be able to take advantage of this opportunity to deeply connect in a way they rarely do otherwise. When they are satisfied by enough closeness, they begin to play and explore in a freer and more pleasurable way that astonishes most observers—including the mother!

Now let's take a look at the stages of your child's development.

PART TWO

Holding Time for You and Your Developing Child

4.

THE SPECIAL ROLES
OF THE PARENTS

The Mothering Role: Why Me?
The Fathering Role: How He?

Mothers often ask me why they have to be the primary person in their child's life. Many women wish that men could share equally in the nurturing of their child, or in some cases take over the mother's role altogether, but the mother is crucial to the child's development, especially in infancy.

No matter how much people try to bring about equality of the sexes, there will remain one stumbling block—biology. While this statement may at first seem sexist, bear with me awhile. Nature has given you extraordinary power as a mother. If you sometimes feel trapped by your responsibility, remember that *holding time* is your safety net. This approach will allow you to deviate a great deal from the traditional pattern of child rearing (mother at home full-time) with fewer deleterious effects.

What *you* need is a strong and enduring, mutually gratifying mother-child attachment. If you have such a bond, you will not wish for your husband to substitute for you. Rather you will find ways for him to nurture you so that you have the resources for sustaining your strong attachment to your child in spite of the stresses from the outside world. You will help your husband to form his own strong and healthy, direct bond with your child. With *holding time* you will find mothering to be one of the most gratifying experiences of your life. And in this context your husband will find fathering to be one of the most gratifying experiences in his life. Why? Because together you will have produced a happy and healthy child who is capable of loving you in return.

The normal development of a child takes place in a social context. That social context for a newborn infant is the mother-child relationship. Recent research demonstrates that newborns a few hours old recognize their own mother's voice and will work (for instance, by sucking hard on a nipple) to achieve the reward of hearing a recording of her voice. They also distinguish their own mother's smell and the appearance of her upper face.

The infant arrives in the world already preferring his mother to all others. However, the survival of the infant depends almost entirely on the strength of his mother's emotional attachment to him. It is known that there is also a biological basis for the mother's attachment to the infant. In fact, there is a sharp change in the mother's hormonal levels just three weeks prior to birth, and women often demonstrate an increase in maternal behavior at that time. Animal studies show why this may be happening. A virgin adult rat will avoid infant rats, but when given a transfusion of blood from a new mother rat, she manifests maternal behavior within fourteen hours. Blood taken from animals before the hormonal shift or more than twenty-four hours after birth has no such effect.

Prolonged early contact between human mother and child has been proven to have positive, sustained effects on the mother-child relationship even years later. On the other hand, separation at the time of birth can have sustained negative effects on the relationship. For example, separation plays a large role in child abuse. A disproportionate number of premature babies who are sent home in good health after prolonged separations necessitated by their specialized care return to the hospital battered and abused by their parents. The mother-child attachment, when it develops normally, is a mutually gratifying connection. It protects both mother and child from the effects of stress in measurable ways.

Everyone knows at least one mother who was completely engrossed in her baby from the moment of birth. The best example I know is Susan. Susan wanted a baby very much. It took her a year and a half to become pregnant. Once pregnant, she was very happy. However, toward the end of her pregnancy she was worried, especially uncomfortable, and preoccupied with physical complaints. To make matters worse, she had a prolonged and particularly painful labor. After twenty-four hours, her son was born. As she lay there uninterested and spent, her baby, who had been quickly wrapped and placed in an isolette, arched his body and turned around until he looked her in the eye. The brief but direct gaze excited her, melted her heart, and bonded her to him at once. As a result of the eye contact that Susan and her baby shared, there was no problem in attachment. Given the circumstances just prior to and during the birth, Susan could have failed to attach to him. (Perinatal events —events around the time of birth—are common precursors of disorders in maternal attachment.) But the moment of eye contact changed Susan's attitude of disinterest and fatigue into exhilaration, and this elevation of spirits set her up for a quick postpartum recovery. Susan's experience is a clear example of the protection from stress afforded by the attachment of mother and infant.

Vicky, on the other hand, did not see her baby at the time of birth. When he was brought to her later, she said she did not know whether he was her baby or not. Attachment occurred along the way, but not as good an attachment as Susan's or as Vicky's attachment with her second child, whom she did see at birth. Throughout his development, Vicky's firstborn showed signs of incomplete attachment. Vicky expressed a marked preference for her second child, from whom there were no separations at birth.

Mary did not see her baby at the time of birth either, because she had an emergency cesarean under general anesthesia. When she awoke, she was informed that she had a large, healthy son. She could hardly believe it, as she had no memory of giving birth. The nurse rolled her past the nursery and pointed to her child, but she could hardly see him without her glasses. She saw him just well enough to recognize her father in his little pink face. Because of complications, her son was not brought to her for twenty-four hours. Then he was not given to her because she was judged to be overmedicated and therefore in no condition to hold him safely. Knowing the importance of early bonding, Mary was heartbroken. Then she became hysterical. After a call to a friend who reminded her about *holding,* she realized that she could compensate for this bad start by extra contact. After a week of almost total separation in the hospital, mother and baby went home together and remained together for the next fifteen months without separation. Mary and her husband decided to have the baby sleep between them. They carried him in a front pack several hours a day. Only the parents and grandparents handled him for the first three months. He became a very happy, contented baby. His subsequent development has been remarkable. He and his mother are well attached. He weaned himself at fifteen months. He moved to his own bed at twenty-eight months. He is very outgoing and curious, and he relates well to parents and peers.

Mary's experience could have led to poor attachment. Fortunately, she and her family knew a great deal about attachment theory and how to apply it. Of course, some lucky families compensate instinctively for early separations, but many do not know how.

There is supportive evidence from animal studies on the effectiveness of forced closeness in cases, such as Mary's, where mother and infant were separated at birth. Sheep and goats separated from their young at birth will reject their own offspring. However, if they are penned together in close quarters for a prolonged time, they will eventually bond nevertheless. The same is true with rats. Studies also show that a period of closeness at birth offsets the traumatic effects of subsequent separations. Mother rats who established closeness immediately following birth will recognize their young and resume their mothering behavior even after a long separation.

An infant's behavior toward the mother is one of the most important determinants of the mother's feelings for and consequent attachment to the child. An alert newborn excites a mother. A baby that does not open its eyes can cause a mother to worry about the baby's chances of survival and make her fearful of attaching. A baby that is soothed by the mother's efforts is pleasing to the mother. A baby that cries no matter what the mother does is frustrating and disappointing. The mother feels ineffectual and alienated—in fact, rejected.

Babies usually give a great many cues. If the mother reads the cues correctly, she will usually be able to meet the baby's needs. Then she will be gratified too. If she misreads the cues, she will have a discontented baby who will only frustrate her. Reading cues is a skill that can be learned even if your own experiences of being mothered left something to be desired.

The smoothest course in the development of a good mother-infant bond goes as follows: The mother is healthy and unstressed throughout the pregnancy. The delivery is normal, short, and with little or no medication so that mother and infant are alert. The two are placed skin to skin seconds after birth and allowed an hour together. Mother and child are together at least several hours a day while in the hospital. Mother remains at home with the child, breast-feeding and caring for the child herself with some help from the father and ideally from the grandparents or a grandparent substitute. Mother has other mothers or the grandmother to help her, to teach her, to offer companionship and support in the early weeks. She learns to respond to the baby's cues accurately and meets his needs. The baby is content. The mother is fulfilled. The attachment is strengthened and sustained.

If we all had our druthers and did not have to face the realities of the economic world, perhaps more of us could have this kind of ideal start with our newborn babies. Since we cannot live in an ideal world, let's try to anticipate and avoid some of the snags or at least strive to offset them by being aware of the way various situations can go awry and how some have been corrected with *holding time.* Imagine that a mother and newborn enjoyed a very good start. Then into this happy scene insert a hired caregiver when the mother must return to her job. The mother feels she has to detach at least a little in order to make this transfer work. By detaching I mean that the mother tries to stop thinking of her presence as essential to her child's well-being and tries to convince herself that he is just as well off in the care of a competent substitute. She tries to be happy when her child is equally responsive to the substitute, despite her normal feeling of possessiveness. These accommodations invariably weaken her attachment to her baby.

Mothers, detaching is not necessary! If a mother maintains as strong a tie to her baby as she possibly can, the baby will be even more able to take love and comfort from the baby-sitter. When the mother allows herself to detach, the baby is less content; the same mutual gratification is not there. The mother may even feel jealous of the care-giver's success with the baby. She says to herself, "Well, I guess I wasn't so important after all." She detaches further, and the care-giver fills in the void even more. As the child grows older, he is more and more responsive to the baby-sitter. The mother feels less and less connected. Often the child will be entirely peaceful with the baby-sitter and then cause an uproar when the mother comes home and the care-giver leaves. Or perhaps the child is only aloof to the mother. In either case, the child is not acting in a way that serves to strengthen the mother-child attachment.

In this theoretical case there was a good mother-child bond at the start. Imagine what happens when a mother and child have a tenuous connection at the time a nanny or baby-sitter is introduced.

I knew a child with such a history. He was an adorable three-and-a-half-year-old whom I had occasion to observe in a tumbling class on a weekly basis. He was insecure and clingy. However, over a two-month period, I saw a change in him. He had a spurt of development in his speech; he seemed happier; he showed much more self-confidence. I decided to ask his nanny if he could come over to play with my son. The nanny said that she would be leaving after that week and I would have to ask his mother. I found out that his mother had been homebound for the previous two months and had enjoyed being with Andy so much that she was taking a year's leave of absence from work to stay home. I laughed at myself for having picked up on the change without suspecting an increase in mother-child attachment. I should have guessed!

We have just looked at a family in which a nanny came between mother and child. Now let's consider another situation, but substitute father for nanny. In a few cases I've seen a father come between mother and child where the result has been more disastrous than with a nanny. Care-givers usually do not go so far as to completely take over the mother's role. Everyone acknowledges the mother. But when the father fills in, the mother often feels preempted, even if the father is only trying to fill a void. Some mothers even become furious with the fathers and grow alienated from both child and father. In some cases, divorces have ensued before the mothers were able to remake a good mother-child attachment. Of course, divorce has also occurred when there was poor or little father-child attachment.

Sue and Peter were married for many years before having a

child. By then Sue had given up hope of becoming pregnant and had embarked on a career. When Renee was born, Sue did not want to stay home. Peter filled the gap. Over a two-year period Sue gradually became more involved with Renee, but she was jealous of the strong tie between Peter and Renee. Nevertheless, the family life was happy. After a few years they decided to have a second child. When Helen was born, Peter did not become at all involved. Sue was hurt and angry. This time she was very involved in the baby's care from the start. Peter was still close to Renee, but despite Sue's efforts he remained aloof from the new baby. The conflict between Sue and Peter over their relationships with the children intensified and spilled over into a deteriorating relationship with each other. Sue decided to divorce Peter. Perhaps if they had had therapy directed toward rebonding appropriately with their children, their marriage could have been saved.

Contrast a similar family. *Holding* was instituted soon after the first baby was born, because the mother complained of the father's usurping her role. The mother was able to establish a strong tie with the baby in the first few months. The father was encouraged to hold the mother as well as the baby. The mother stopped feeling jealous of the strong father-child tie because she felt her own strong mother-child tie and her improved tie with her husband. When they had their second child, both became as strongly attached to the new baby as they had to the first. They avoided both parental and sibling rivalry in the first child. They are a happy family still using *holding time. Holding time* simply forces people to relate to one another and to their children and forces their children to relate to them.

In the case of Darlene and Ron, both parents were strongly attached to their first little girl. But once again the mother felt jealous of the father-child relationship, in this case mainly because the father gave a great deal of attention to the baby and very little to the mother. Nevertheless all went relatively well for the first two years. Then the mother became pregnant accidentally. Neither parent was ready for a second child. When the baby was born, the first child became intensely jealous. The parents placated her by ignoring the baby, a quiet, undemanding infant who just slept whenever put in the crib.

The second child did not develop well. When I first saw the baby at seven months, she was completely withdrawn, immobile, and unresponsive. *Holding* therapy was begun; the younger child's development is proceeding, and the older child's sibling rivalry has been markedly reduced. The mother now feels a stronger attachment to both children. Mother and father are working on their relationship.

The degree to which a father should be involved in a nurturing role is highly individual. For some mothers, the traditional fathering role with little direct father-child contact is acceptable, as long as the father supports the mother-child attachment. For other mothers, ample direct father-child contact is mandatory. Some stay-at-home mothers need fathers to take over the minute they arrive home. However, when this mix works, the mother does not see the father's involvement as substitute mothering or as competitive. Rather, she sees herself as the primary figure and the father as welcome relief.

To say that fathers should not be mothers in no way diminishes the importance of the father's role. The father is as important as the mother. How mother and father cooperate to successfully create a nurturing home can vary widely from couple to couple.

Kathleen and Cal are an example of a couple whose lifestyle worked well in the early years of their family life. Cal traveled all week, returning home on weekends. While he was away he called nightly. He brought Kathleen gifts and showered her with attention when he came home. Because he worked out of town, he had no work obligations on the weekend. He was entirely free for family life whenever at home. Kathleen felt secure and happy.

After their second child was born, Cal went into business for himself. He no longer traveled, but he worked seven days a week. Kathleen expected the support and attention during the week that she had been used to receiving on the weekend. Because he had been so devoted whenever he was at home, she expected more of the same daily. Instead, she got less. She became hurt, angry, disappointed. Her nurturing of her second child was disturbed by these changes in the family. The child became a problem. The older child, too, experienced difficulties. The marriage almost dissolved before they regained their balance. The change in the father's input had had a severe effect on the mother. This situation again illustrates how changes in the internal balance of the family and the family interactions can interfere with the bonding of parents to one another and to their children and the bonding of children to their parents.

Jody and Bill are a couple whose child-rearing practices followed the traditional pattern: the mother took care of home and children; the father took care of business and finances. Both were satisfied with this arrangement. But multiple corporate moves challenged the family's stability. The children's development was affected. *Holding time* was instituted between mother and children and between mother and father. Bill became more involved in child rearing. Bill and Jody got closer to each other. The children's development improved dramatically.

Children survive many different traumas. But survival is a poor alternative to optimal development. A strong, healthy, and enduring attachment between mother and child is the basis for optimal development. Even good nurturing by another relative cannot approach the effectiveness of the mother-child bond.

Jill and Ryan separated when their son, John, was three. Ryan's mother took over John's care after Jill's boyfriend mistreated the child. Jill did not see John for the next eight years. He was brought to me because he was experiencing peer difficulties and was doing poorly in school. I suggested John see his mother, and as a result Jill and Ryan came to a session together with John. A joyful reunion took place in my office. Jill began to see John on a regular basis. John's peer relations improved immediately, and his school performance improved gradually. He is now a college student on partial scholarship at a major university. This boy had been raised in the loving home of his paternal grandparents. Yet it was the renewed relationship with his mother that put him back on the path to good development.

Hilary provides an extreme example of the need for a good mother-child bond. She was placed in a mental institution at age nineteen after a suicide attempt. At the time of her hospitalization her parents were separated; it was their fourth separation in a five-year period. Hilary had been living with her father, with whom she had a reasonably good relationship. She was estranged from her mother.

Hilary's mother, Jo, had come to me for her own depression. I explained to her that a mother does not usually do well herself when her child is in serious trouble. I asked her to return home, reconcile with her husband, Ron, and sign Hilary out of the mental institution. Jo felt betrayed by me. She had at long last extricated herself from an unhappy twenty-year marriage and finally had a life and career of her own. I insisted that she meet these requirements in order to enter into therapy with me. She agreed. The next week she brought Hilary and Ron to the session. It went well. That night Hilary slit both wrists—*slightly*. The local emergency room called me to see if I would accept responsibility for the patient. I declined, saying that the mother was the only one who could. Jo agreed. The next week, after our session, Hilary slit one wrist in a token fashion. From that day on, Jo remained with Hilary for five months, twenty-four hours a day. They had several hours of *holding time* daily. Ron and Jo also had daily *holding*. A younger daughter, Ann, who had been neglected because of the family problems, had daily *holding* as well. Hilary got well, became independent, was able to hold a responsible job for the first time in her life, and got married. Jo and Ron became a happily married couple for the first time in twenty years.

This family had disintegrated almost totally. *Holding time* allowed them to attain a level of mutually gratifying relationships that they had not previously achieved. As Hilary put it, "You can't really leave home successfully until home is good. You will be looking for mothers and fathers in your male-female relationships for the rest of your life if you don't get it together, especially with your mother, before you leave home."

Ann, the younger sister, said, "*Holding* is like an insurance policy, even for families that aren't having overtly difficult problems, as we did. My sister was suicidal, but it was more like she would have done anything to get attention—anything. She was screaming for years, and it just became worse and worse and worse. 'Pay attention to me. Be my parents. Give me something.'"

Hilary added, "Wouldn't it be nice to go away from home with your parents' blessings and their presence and their peace of mind and your peace of mind in knowing that you can come back any time and have a real tight relationship?"

Hilary's case history illustrates how the mother's relationship to the child and the father's support of that connection can positively affect the child's development. From Hilary's history and the other examples a pattern emerges. Disturbances in mother-child attachment cause problems, either in the mother, the child, the marriage, or all three. Repair of the mother-child bond improves all three.

If you can achieve a strong, healthy, mutually gratifying mother-child bond, you will find mothering to be one of the most rewarding experiences of your life. You will want to share the experience with your husband, but you will never want to relinquish that primacy that makes possible optimal child as well as family development.

The role of the father is different from the role of the mother. There is a saying: "The most important thing a father can do for his children is to love their mother." The reality that the mother's bond with the child is primary in no way diminishes the importance of the father. Mother-child bonding occurs with or without a father. However, the father is crucial for sustaining the attachment. Mother-child *holding* has proven to be useful and sometimes curative in a variety of childhood psychological disturbances. However, the improvement has been dramatic only in those cases in which the father not only loved the mother, as the saying suggests, but also did *holding* with her and participated actively in the mother-child *holding*. This unanticipated finding was confirmed by five years of correlation between fathers' attitudes and participation on the one hand and results of treatment on the other. Nothing else seemed to account for the different results; the only consistent variable was the father. Children with involved fathers recovered from their emotional problems quickly, while those whose fathers were not involved improved slowly. Children without fathers improved only a little and very, very slowly. The children whose fathers would not participate improved at first and then reached a plateau and did not make further progress. Once this difference was made obvious, some of the fathers were brought in. Their children then improved further. The disturbed children who have never reached a cure are those whose fathers have remained uninvolved. You may wonder why I am emphasizing the cases with problem children in discussing the role of the father. The reason is that the role of the father with normal children has not been studied as much as it has in cases of disturbed children, but the principles are the same.

Studies have shown that the absence of fathers is common in children, particularly boys, with learning problems and a history of juvenile delinquency. Other studies have shown the type of fathering that produces well-adjusted, competent children. The formula for success is a benevolent, interested, involved, non-authoritarian, nurturing father and a nurturing, positively reinforcing mother. In order for a mother to sustain her nurturing, she must be reinforced, buoyed up, refueled by her husband. She also needs him to take over for her at times.

One mother poignantly illustrated these needs when during *holding time* she yelled at her son for punching his father. She said, "If any harm comes to your father, I will be no use to you. I am no good without your father." Her husband was a good father. He had always worked hard to provide financial comfort for the family, yet he always found time for his wife and children. He helped her with the chores and did a great deal of the cooking. He was also in touch with her on a feeling level. If she cried, he comforted her. If the children disobeyed, he reinforced her position. If they hurt her, he defended her. Best of all, he loved her and showed it clearly with words and with displays of affection. The mother had had a very sad childhood, with early loss of her mother. Mothering did not come naturally. However, with her husband's help she had become a good and fulfilled mother. This father provided the safe environment for happy family relationships.

Our cousins, the great apes, exhibit the same need for fathers. Chimp fathers provide a safe environment for nurturing; they represent benign but vigilant authority and maintain a vigorously playful relationship with the offspring.

A profoundly psychotic mother once came into my office with two very well functioning children. It was hard to imagine how these children's needs had been met, considering the state of the mother. After observing the family, it became clear that the children looked to the father for permission to do things, to have their noses wiped, whatever. They seemed very content, even though the mother really was not functioning. The whole story was revealed when the mother left the room to go to the toilet. The children became frantic. They could not make use of their father unless their mother was present. Because their ties to their mother were strained by her psychotic state, they had severe separation anxiety. With both parents present, they could make use of what each of them could give. This example underscores the primary role of the mother, but it also demonstrates to what extent a father's efforts to provide a nurturing environment can succeed in stabilizing even a family with a nonfunctional mother so that the children are able to extract enough nurturing to develop normally.

The mother who told her son she would be no use to him without the father was far from psychotic, but because she had had little mothering in her own childhood, she could not have done a good job without the nurturing environment created by the father.

Children learn to control their impulses as they develop. The main impetus at first is that this self-control makes their parents happy and approving. (Eventually children internalize the wish for self-control.) Early in life it is mainly the mother who provides the motivation. However, as the children grow older, the father becomes increasingly important. First of all, children become aware of outside danger. Their idealized view of a powerful Daddy helps them to feel protected from all danger. You have heard kids say, "My dad can lift anything," or, "My dad can beat your dad, so you better not mess with me." More important, this view of Daddy as the ultimate power protects the child from his own impulses. Limits are necessary to a child's sense of security.

Another area where the father is crucial is gender identification. Apparently the father is the one who most encourages a boy to be manly and a girl to be feminine. Some may think that role stereotyping should be stopped in an egalitarian society. This would be a mistake, because for ultimate fulfillment in relationships, men need to feel masculine and women need to feel feminine. Proper gender identification in no way condemns a woman to lack of success in the outside world or a man to lack of success in relationships. Being comfortable with yourself helps in the world of business and in the realm of intimate relationships. If you are trying to stifle feminine identification in a girl or masculine identification in a boy, you are jeopardizing their acceptance of themselves, which will in turn damage their ability to relate to others. Boys and girls are different. Enjoy the differences in your children, and they will enjoy them too. We need men and women who can love each other and become mutually interdependent. We do not need fathers to be mothers or vice versa. A child needs a mother doing the mothering job and a father doing the fathering job. There is enough latitude in each role to guarantee job satisfaction if each accepts himself and the other for what he or she is. The father's interactions with his children can stimulate this kind of healthy development.

Fathers are equally important as role models for girls and for boys. Boys pattern themselves after their fathers. The father becomes the model for the girl's choice of husband, regardless of whether the family life is satisfactory or not. In addition, girls copy some characteristics of their fathers, just as boys do (and just as boys in some ways copy their mothers). When all goes well, these are useful identifications. When there are problems, children often copy the problem behavior. Sometimes children reject negative parental patterns and, reacting blindly, try to change them in their own lives, only to discover that they have done the same thing in another guise—or something worse.

The feelings brought up during *holding time* also tell parents what patterns are being perceived and copied. Therefore, you have a better chance to correct now what is happening in your child's development. In addition, you as the parent have a chance to reevaluate your own behavior. Once you gain this awareness, you have a much greater chance of controlling what you do. You can decide how you wish to behave instead of merely being a victim of your past. Awareness can help you to be the best father or mother possible.

Even though mothers and fathers have different roles, both are essential to their child's healthy development. Luckily for everyone, each role has its special gratifications.

5.

THE EXPECTANT MOTHER
AND THE GROWING FETUS
How to Get Ready for Mothering

Pregnancy is a very important time in the bonding process for the expectant mother and for the growing fetus as well. You may be surprised to learn that bonding happens during pregnancy. Actually, I believe that future mother-child bonding is even influenced by the childhood experience of the mother as she identifies with her own mother and develops a desire to become a mother herself. Doll play reinforces this: the little girl practices what she sees and fantasizes about being a mother. She builds on these fantasies throughout her development. Of course, her experience of being mothered is a key element in the pattern she develops. The meaning of motherhood for her is largely drawn from her perception of her own mother's mothering. This principle is important to remember when you are mothering your child, for you are determining what kind of parent your child will be.

In any case, the little girl grows up with fantasies of what it will be like to become a mother. The fact that most women wish to be mothers at some point in their lives bespeaks the power of their mothers' examples. Many women even wish to have the same number of children their mothers had. This pattern is particularly common in women with positive feelings about their upbringing. Some find themselves having a first child at the same age as their mothers did, regardless of feeling positive or negative about their childhood. It is helpful to think about your own fantasies and wishes for motherhood. Talk about them with your mother when you are pregnant. Ask your mother about her experience of being pregnant with you. Find out what misconceptions you may have had about her experience of her mothering. Awareness of these ideas often helps you to respond freely to your own pregnancy and imminent motherhood; you will avoid becoming a slave to misconceptions or automatic reactions from your past that will interfere with your pleasure and healthy function as a mother.

Hormones have a profound effect on how you feel during your pregnancy, and this in turn affects your bonding with your baby. Some women really enjoy pregnancy as a euphoric state. They luxuriate in being slowed down both physically and mentally. Their thoughts turn inward. They are preoccupied with their bodies, with their feelings, with thoughts of the baby. This happy reaction to her physical state can help a woman bond with her unborn child. I think that the old custom of confinement during pregnancy may have been instituted to help a woman indulge herself in a positive way and that the bonding process was promoted by the vegetative state of pregnancy. The woman was catered to, waited on, and protected. Today if a woman is too preoccupied with herself, she can end up feeling cut off from everyone else.

The hormonal changes can also have a negative effect. If she likes to be in control, her pregnancy can cause some serious conflict because now she cannot control her body. Her body changes at first in ways she can't always detect, but after a while the changes can be felt inside and out. If a woman is trying to stay in control or trying to get work accomplished, these changes can be experienced as an intrusion. If a woman reacts negatively to the changes, this will have a harmful effect on her bonding with the unborn child. On the other hand, if she luxuriates in these changes, then this helps her to bond.

If you are one of the women who might respond negatively to the pregnant state, perhaps knowing more about what is going on inside you would help you to enjoy it. Books about pregnancy could be helpful, especially those with photos of the fetus at various stages of development. For example, if you know that the hormones that cause morning sickness are the chemicals that help the fetus implant on the wall of the uterus and stay there, you might marvel at morning sickness despite its misery. Excitement over the events taking place inside you might ease you through the rough period. Knowing that hormones can make you excitable and weepy will keep you from thinking you are going crazy. Instead you may say, "Oh, there's the emotional instability caused by the hormones of pregnancy." It won't feel like a surprise attack from outside.

There are recent studies that reveal how the fetus functions as a feeling being. What is most exciting is a study suggesting that the fetus reacts to a stimulus in the same way an adult does. When stimulation is applied to the mother's belly, the fetal heart rate speeds up several seconds before the fetus begins to move, just as an adult's heart rate accelerates during contemplation of action. Whether the fetus is actually thinking or not we may never know, but we are safer in assuming that unborn and newborn infants are perceiving, feeling beings than in assuming they are not. If we assume an unborn child feels and hears, we will act in a more careful way in its presence. Start talking to it. (Some people talk more to a pet than they do to an infant!) Pregnancy is the best time to begin habits that you want to carry on after the baby is born. In the meantime, your baby will be conditioned to your voice and will be much more soothed by it after birth.

Mothers have noticed that a fetus will respond to music by increased or decreased movement. After birth, the babies respond in a similar way to the music they heard in utero. Similar reports come from mothers who read to the baby before birth. There are even extreme reports suggesting that a baby remembers the content of traumatic conversations heard while still in utero. In any case, a fetus's hearing is acute enough so that excessive noises can damage it.

Special nerve cells in the forebrain play a role in memory. If these neurons are lost, memory goes. These neurons are not normally functional early in life, but perhaps children who report fetal memories had these special cells functioning before their usual time. Whether a fetus remembers is still unknown. What is certain is that the mother's upset causes changes in her body that affect the fetus. For example, when her heart rate increases, the fetus can hear and feel the accelerated beat. Also, if the mother's stress hormones are released, they affect the fetus.

The brain of the fetus is complex from the beginning. This is no surprise. What is surprising is that nerve cell division is completed between sixteen and twenty weeks after conception. After that period, your child will never make new neurons. This is why you must not take drugs of any kind during early pregnancy. Otherwise you risk interfering with the nerve cell formation of your baby. Although no new nerve cells grow after this period, millions of new connections between nerve cells will be established in the next twenty years.

Your job is to make sure that your baby's environment is the best possible for making cell connections. During pregnancy, that means eating well to provide the vitamins, minerals, and nutrients needed for all growth. An example of the importance of nutrition is the zinc requirement: low zinc is associated with retardation. Another example is the effect of alcohol and nicotine. Both are associated with low birth weight, which is in turn associated with medical complications.

When a mother has a negative attitude about pregnancy, she generally takes poor care of herself. Poor prenatal care is associated with premature births as well as with bonding failure. When a mother takes good care of herself, she feels she is doing something good for her baby. This satisfaction enhances the mother's bond to the baby.

Since mother-child attachment is already taking place during pregnancy, everything that you can do to make that time a positive experience will help you bond. Things that will enhance bonding include:

1. Improving your relationship with your parents. If you are close, become closer. If you have problems, try to overcome them now. Reach out. At every phase of development (your pregnancy is one), you have a new opportunity for emotional growth as well as for resolution of unsettled issues. Your parents are more open at this time also, since they are becoming grandparents, a distinct phase in *their* development.

2. Enjoying more closeness with your husband, the key man in the support of your mothering role.

3. Taking good care of yourself and therefore your growing fetus by resting, eating well, and avoiding drugs, cigarettes, alcohol, and emotional upsets.

4. Talking to your growing unborn baby. Stimulate your baby by rocking, talking, singing, reading aloud, playing music, moving your belly with your hands.

5. Reviewing your past and present so that your awareness will prevent unresolved conflicts from interfering with your parenting.

6. Building a support system with other pregnant women or mothers with newborns so that you will not be alone in your mothering. Natural-childbirth classes and La Leche League, a mothers' breast-feeding group, are two good sources of people.

7. Learning about breast feeding. Discover how to do it at least part of the time, even if you plan to work soon after giving birth.

Of course the family members' reactions to the pregnancy can enhance or diminish the mother's tendency to bond. For example, if the father is not interested in the pregnancy, the mother can experience feelings of isolation and then become angry at the unborn child. Or if the father is thrilled, the mother feels proud of being pregnant and attached to the baby. When the father likes to feel the baby kick and when he talks to the baby, the mother receives attention too. The baby is then the cause of the mother-father interaction, and his positive response fosters her greater attachment. Or if the maternal grandmother feels excited about her daughter's pregnancy, there is a stronger mother-fetus bond. The opposite can occur too.

Kendra was bewildered when her mother rejected her pregnancy. For no apparent reason, she wanted Kendra to give the baby up for adoption, even though Kendra and her husband were happy about the pregnancy. When the baby was born, Kendra felt unable to mother him. She said that she felt she could not pick him up even when he cried, and for the most part she did not. The baby gradually withdrew. Later, when the grandmother was roped into therapy with Kendra and her child, they worked on their feelings about the child and their relationship. Kendra began to respond more normally to the child, and his withdrawal was arrested and eventually reversed.

The best insurance that you will have good prenatal bonding is increased closeness with the father and with your own mother and father. Try to increase your awareness of your need for them. Once you accept your need, try to communicate it in a positive way. Engage them in conversations about your pregnancy. Learn about fetal development and share your knowledge with them. Learn about childbirth. Ask your husband and your parents to participate. Talk with your mother about her pregnancy. Talk with your mother-in-law about hers. It will help you to learn that you are not alone in your experience. Talk to other mothers too.

Be sure to learn about cesarean births as well as natural childbirth. Delivery by cesarean section occurs in about 20 percent of births in the United States. Just in case you may have to have a C-section, read about it. It is a very safe method for the child, although it is stressful for you. If you are prepared for it, it can be a good experience. Discuss the possibility with your husband and your parents.

Figure out what you want to do about feeding. Breast feeding is thought to provide the best nutrition as well as the closest bond between mother and child. Some women feel that they want their husbands to share in feeding the baby. This wish can be carried out even if you are breast-feeding. You can pump and store your milk. This extra supply can be fed to the baby by your husband or anyone else you choose.

Breast milk confers important immunities on the baby and may help prevent allergies, especially if the baby does not eat other food until he is eight or nine months old. Mothers who are planning to return to work often decline to breast-feed because it would only be for a short time. For immunological purposes alone, it may be worth the trouble. For bonding considerations, it may be even more important in view of the separations work will bring. It has recently been found that there is a hormone, an opiumlike substance many times stronger than morphine, released by the pancreas of both mother and baby during breast feeding. The feelings of contentment and well-being resulting from this pleasure hormone may foster the natural bond of affection and trust between mother and baby.

La Leche League is a mothers' group that helps educate prospective mothers about breast feeding. If you do breast-feed, they will help you, both practically and emotionally. If you are not going to breast-feed, be ready to simulate the closeness of the experience. Think about holding your newborn baby close to you, preferably skin to skin, the way you would if you were breast-feeding. It is very important to allow yourself and your baby to be close and to gaze into each other's eyes during this time of gratifying his hunger. The distance between your faces when the baby is resting at your breast is the ideal distance for newborns to focus. In order for optimal eye use to develop, this mother-infant gazing is apparently very important for the first six months.

Pregnancy is the best time to think about how you will handle the first few exhausting postpartum months. Begin even sooner if you can. Start to think about your baby while you are trying to become pregnant. The average American woman takes eighteen months to conceive. That gives you a real head start on forming your image of motherhood.

Mary had two miscarriages and then did not become pregnant for eighteen months. During that time she asked herself, "Would I rather go jogging or be pregnant? Would I rather go to a concert or be pregnant? Would I rather be doing this work or be pregnant?" By the time she became pregnant, she was ready for the completely inactive pregnancy that her doctor prescribed. While pregnant, she not only gloried in the state of pregnancy and its joyful expectation, but also began to anticipate the time when the baby would be in her arms. By the time the baby was born, she was emotionally prepared for the demands of a newborn. She had experienced more than two years of psychological preparation for caring for this baby. She had had more than two years of bonding with the imagined infant by the time he arrived. I might add that she had also prepared herself for a C-section just in case, and she had a positive attitude about it because she had learned about the benefits to the baby. Also she knew that she might have to compensate for the lack of bonding at the moment of birth. Because of all this preparation, Mary was able to bond well with her baby and to give him the extra care required to overcome extensive separations in the first week of life caused by the baby's treatment for jaundice.

If you have other children, pregnancy is the time to work on becoming closer with them so that their negative reaction to sharing you with a newborn will be minimized. Often a mother begins to withdraw from an older child during pregnancy, partly because of the physical effects of pregnancy itself and partly because of the notion that the child must grow up in a hurry to make room for the new baby. *Withdrawal is a mistake.* Instead, force yourself to be even more attentive to and intimate with your child. Extra attention will fortify him against the drop he will unavoidably feel when the new baby comes home. Baby him. Show him that you know how to meet his needs. Most children regress when a new baby comes or is on the way. A natural inclination is to try to talk him out of his distress. Don't. Satisfy his longings to be in that special place. When his needs are met, he will prefer to be on his appropriate level of development. Talk to him about his feelings. If you can accept his negative feelings, they will not be so scary to him. He will let you help him deal with them. If his feelings do not alienate you, then he will feel safe. If he is safe in his connection with you, he need not fear a newcomer. He will then be free to enjoy the new baby as much as an older child can enjoy a baby. This is a limited amount. Do not try to talk him into enjoying it. Let it happen naturally. It will if he is not losing out to the baby.

Use your pregnancy to solidify your connection with all of your family. You will help pave the way for a happy family setting into which to bring a new baby.

6.

THE EXHAUSTED MOTHER AND THE DEMANDING INFANT

*How to Get You and Your Baby
Off to a Good Start*

The moment of childbirth is extremely important to the formation of a strong attachment between you and your baby. Beforehand, try to arrange with your doctor to have some time immediately after birth for you and your husband to be alone with the baby. Put the baby on your body, skin to skin. If the birth conditions do not allow this immediately, do it as soon as possible. Each time you pick up your baby for feeding, unwrap him. Put him on you skin to skin. Once home from the hospital, carry him in a front pack as much as possible. Sleep with him between you and your husband. Talk to your baby as much as possible. Look into his eyes. Hold him close when you feed him.

Comfort your baby as soon as he shows signs of distress. You can't do too much. No amount of gentle handling is too much. You can only spoil your baby in one way: by not meeting his needs. To develop trust, you must meet his needs. If you do, he will be well attached to you. *He will trust and love you. He will be content. Your life will be easier.*

Parenting a new baby is a complex task. In looking at all that a parent brings to this task, it is important to consider each parent's own family background. Studies have shown that parents establish attachments with their children according to their history of attachment with their own parents. The exceptions are parents who have examined their pasts and who have therefore been able, when necessary, to alter their patterns of relating. Even accidents of fate such as one's own birth order can have a profound effect on attachment with a particular child. For example, if you are a father whose little sister got all your parents' positive attention, then fathering a little girl may cause you intense distress.

Such a situation occurred in Joe's family. He and his mother suffered a severe bonding disorder because of a two-week separation quickly followed by a one-month separation, all in the first two months of life. Joe and his mother never made up for this separation. When Joe's sister was born, she and their mother bonded very well. Joe tried hard to attract positive attention by always striving to be a good child and an excellent student. He became a good doctor. When he married later in life, he hoped for a son. His secret wish was to compensate for his sad childhood by giving a son the attention he had never had. When his daughter was born, he was very disappointed. His wife could not understand why he was always trying to keep her from paying attention to their daughter. Whenever Joe interacted with the daughter, it was in a way fathers normally treat sons. The daughter expressed a strong wish at a very early age to be a boy. Her father's approval was given only when she acted like a boy. This is a rather obvious case of a father's past interfering. You may not know how you are living out your past unless you really take a close look.

Jill is a more subtle example. She was overindulgent with her daughter. She was not treated that way as a child, and she did not recognize the fact that she was reacting against her past. Jill had felt so uncared for by a mother who was never home, because she was out doing good works, that she wanted to give her own daughter all the love and attention she felt she had missed. She saw her indulgent behavior as loving. Her daughter felt the insecurity of not having limits set for her and saw it as lack of involvement. If they had not had help, the daughter would have gone on feeling unloved and would have been out of control as well. Overindulgence is not the same as closeness.

Mothers and fathers can avoid this pitfall somewhat by discussing their pasts with each other. You can tell each other your feelings about your parents, how they treated you, how you wished they had treated you, what things you would do the same with your children, what things you would do differently. It would be wonderful if you could discuss the same topics with your parents. You may find out that your perceptions of the past are different from your parents' perceptions of the same events and practices. Often when prospective parents discuss these topics openly with their own parents, they see things in a new way that helps them to forgive some of the hurt they felt. Forgiveness helps them to interrupt the automatic repetition of patterns or the equally dangerous reaction of doing the opposite of what they think was done to them, and to choose a path that meets the needs of parent and child in the present without the burden of feelings from the past.

A common idea is that mothering comes naturally. As I've said before, what comes naturally is mothering the way you were mothered. If it was good, you are fortunate. If it wasn't good, you now have a chance to do better. There is nothing wrong with gaining the satisfaction that you missed as a child from having your own child parented better. Just make sure that what you do really is better.

Another factor to consider is the current marital relationship. Often parents are so sidetracked by the work of caring for an infant that they don't have a chance to think about each other. Now more than ever you need to think about each other and to talk with each other. Mothers need a great deal of support, nurturing, love, tenderness, and companionship from fathers to refuel them when they are mothering a newborn. The hormonal upheaval on top of the sleep deprivation makes mothers very fragile during this period. A father is in a precarious position too. He has just experienced a loss or at least a diminution of the attention he had been receiving from his wife. To make matters worse, he is required to give more than ever to his wife and to the new baby as well. And he too is sleeping less.

If the father participated in the birth process, he is better equipped to handle this large order because he is more attached to the baby than had he not been present. Natural-childbirth classes in which the father participates before delivery help him to attach even if later it turns out that he cannot be present at the birth, for example with some C-sections. The more the father participates in taking care of the mother before and during the birth and of the mother and child after the birth, the more attachment is fostered between father and child and usually between father and mother as well. This attachment with the father is crucial for many reasons.

One is that it helps reinforce the mother's attachment to the child. Other people's interest in the baby is a potent factor in reinforcing a mother's attachment to him. In fact, a study of mother-child interaction proved that the mother's nurturing improved just by virtue of being studied. Another positive result of good father-child and mother-father attachment is the reduction of the father's jealousy or feelings of being left out of the developing love affair between mother and infant. Father-mother attachment has proven to be the key element in retrieving children when development founders. It is safe to assume that it is also a key element in development that proceeds optimally.

The baby is best cared for if allowed to sleep with the parents. Fathers who are very attached to their child are more apt to allow or even to welcome having the baby sleep in the parental bed. Sleeping with the baby is easiest if the baby is placed on a cloth attached to two bolsters. The baby can be placed on the cloth between the bolsters to keep him from rolling into the parents. People often worry about crushing the baby in their sleep. Don't worry. Babies squawk when you bump them. The only problem is the baby's inching over to you and waking *you* up.

No matter how happy you are to have a new baby, it is hard work and a big adjustment. However, life at this stage is much easier if you have a contented, happy baby who is responsive to your comforting actions. You are probably saying to yourself, "Great, if that's the kind of baby you were given." A common assumption is that babies are born one way or another: easy or fussy, cuddly or avoiding, wanting to be held or liking to be left alone in a crib. Do not believe this. Studies have shown that extra massage, tender loving care, and extra holding turn cranky babies into easy babies, and standard hospital nursery care can turn an easy baby into a cranky one. In fact, if colicky babies are held more, their colicky periods are reduced.

Another study has shown that carrying an infant over your shoulder promotes alertness that in turn prevents the apnea or nonbreathing periods which are associated with sudden infant death. In addition, other researchers say that infants who sleep next to their mothers are "reminded" to breathe when the mother breathes. They even breathe in synchrony.

In any case, it is safe to conclude that our love and care can affect a baby. We need not condemn an irritable infant to remaining so. And we should not allow a contented baby to slide into irritability.

At last, most experts agree that an infant's needs should be met as quickly and as completely as humanly possible. We now know that it is important to respond to any distress signal with swift intervention to avoid the risk of damaging a baby's sense of trust in the care-givers. Instead of "spoiling" a baby, this quick attention to his needs develops the security that will make him less frantic when he later has to learn to wait for some things. It is difficult to jump whenever the baby complains. But if you realize that there is something in it for you, it will be easier to do. You will have a more contented baby in the present and a happier, better-adjusted child later if you do your best to respond immediately to his signals.

Signals are sent to you in many ways. Crying is a universally recognizable signal. However, there are different kinds of cries. Try to listen for differences. Try to associate what was wrong with the sound of the crying. When your baby cries, pick him up. Talk to him. If he is dry and well fed but still crying, he may want contact. Cuddle him. Coo to him. Most babies will become content. If your baby still is not content, hold him more tightly. Rock him. Stroke him. Continue to hold him. Walk around with him, still holding him tightly. Do not stop until your baby is cuddly and content. Sometimes babies have to learn to make use of comforting. Very often extremely intelligent babies withdraw because they feel overwhelmed. They would rather withdraw than take comfort from a care-giver. It is much better for such a baby to learn to be comforted early on, even if it takes some extra effort, than for him to learn a pattern of withdrawal.

Remember that our species would not have survived if babies did not learn to take comfort from their mothers and to mold to their bodies and go to sleep despite the mothers' vigorous walking or even toiling. Everyone has seen films or photos of healthy, peaceful babies being carried on their mother's bodies in tribal societies; they look either very alert and curious or very content and sleepy. *You cannot hold or carry an infant too much.* The risk facing you is that your baby will have too little holding and carrying.

You can compensate partially for too little holding by massaging your infant three or four times a day with baby oil and by giving his joints passive movement. Move your baby's arms and legs all around. Make him bend his legs at the hip, knee, and ankles, his arms at the shoulder, elbow, and wrist. Move his toes and fingers. Gently turn his head. Jiggle his tummy with your hand. Kiss his tummy. Look into his eyes. Infants like to make eye contact. Looking into your baby's eyes enhances your developing attachment.

When you feed your baby, either by nursing or with a bottle, hold him close to your chest and look into his eyes. Make sounds. Talk to him. Many mothers don't talk to their infants because they think it is too soon for the baby to understand the words. I have seen seriously delayed speech in a very bright four-year-old that was largely the result of his mother's not speaking to him during most of the first two years of life. In fact, in the first year the baby takes in the whole foundation of language, including and especially grammar and syntax. If you don't speak to him directly, it is somewhat more difficult for him to learn language. Of course, if he overhears other people's conversations, he will learn. Nevertheless, we should do all we can to stimulate language acquisition. Speaking to a baby is a way of maintaining contact, and it becomes particularly important when you are near him but not holding him. Since children learn from watching and listening long before they can physically take an action, tell your baby what you are doing and how you are doing it. This kind of contact will help you feel connected as much as it makes your baby feel connected and comforted.

Many people think an infant is not aware of what is going on in his environment. Studies being done now are revealing previously unimagined sensitivity and responsiveness in newborns, such as recognizing their mother's voices and smells and showing signs of withdrawal even with as little as one hour's separation from the mother. Much is made of the infant's inability to see. In fact, by fourteen weeks an infant has near-mature visual capacity. By this time he can focus at all distances, but even soon after birth, he can recognize your face.

Infants do look around; they listen to their own sounds as well as other sounds; they mouth objects; they exercise their head and limbs; they give signals to their mother about their needs. They are capable of expressing anger when they are uncomfortable. However, if the mother responds to small signals, even infants will learn to wait to have their needs met. Rage is the response to discomfort of a baby who does not expect to be rescued. Many of the milestones of development described for babies and children are reached earlier by babies who are carried on the mother's body, spoken to a great deal, massaged, rocked, and kept in the parents' bed at night. In contrast, babies who spend most of their time in carriages, strollers, plastic infant seats, and cribs generally reach the milestones later.

Mother-child attachment is fostered by giving the infant a feeling of being loved and cared for through constant gentle handling. It is not overstimulating for an infant to be carried in a mother's arms or on her body in a baby carrier. You cannot overdo meeting an infant's needs. Prompt response to signals leads to greater attachment, as does talking to your baby, lying with him skin to skin, gazing into his eyes, cuddling, sleeping with him, and carrying him on your body. Babies do not need quiet in order to sleep. If your baby is easily awakened by slight noises, carry him in a baby carrier or on your chest for several hours a day. Your baby will become calmer and less irritable. He will learn to sleep in the midst of raucous noise or tipped upside down while you are scrubbing the floor. If your baby is colicky, carry him more. A study showed that just three hours of carrying a day cut babies' colicky periods in half. If you use a front baby pack, you can go about your activities while carrying your baby.

If you and your baby were separated at the time of birth, you can compensate for it now by extra contact. It takes months to make up for the effects of early separation. The more you can be with your baby, the more you will overcome any negative effects of the birth experience on your attachment.

If you did not see your baby at birth or if you have an adopted baby, you need extra contact to ensure bonding. The best way to compensate is to go to bed with the baby for a few days. It is interesting that some primitive tribes have just such a custom for all mothers of newborns. The mother and baby are put in a hammock and are waited on for several days. Put your baby on your chest, skin to skin. Talk to him. Look into his eyes. Let him sleep on your chest. Just a few days of this practice will go a long way toward establishing a strong attachment. In addition, you will find that you have a contented, easily comforted, responsive baby. On your part, you will be much more attuned to your baby's signals and therefore much more adept at responding accurately and quickly. So many mothers are anxious, especially with their first child because they have never had any experience with a newborn. Strong attachment with its resulting mutual responsiveness more than makes up for lack of experience.

In fact, any time in the first few months when things are not going well, if your baby is irritable or if you feel exhausted and unraveled, stay in bed with your baby until you both feel better. So often mothers are told to go out to dinner or to take some time away from the baby. This rarely works. In fact, it usually aggravates the situation by making the mother feel guilty for needing time off and anxious because she failed to function the way she expected. It makes the baby more anxious because he gets even less of what he needs—close contact with his mother. It is a downward spiral. Whenever you wonder what course of action to take, ask yourself what effect it will have on your mother-child attachment. Try to do what you think will strengthen attachment.

Exercise is very important in rebuilding your strength and restoring your chemistry after you've given birth and when you are deprived of sleep. Try to schedule regular exercise. If you do not like other forms of exercise, at least walk. Walking briskly is actually one of the best forms of exercise. Put your baby in a front pack and take him along. You will feel better. You will sleep better.

Whether you are breast-feeding or not, watch your diet. Your body needs to replenish its supplies after a pregnancy. Good nutrition will speed your postpartum recovery. If you are breast-feeding, be sure to take in adequate protein as well as minerals and vitamins.

You may wonder how to carry out all the suggestions in this chapter when you are already exhausted and stretched to your limit. You will find that these suggestions will turn out to be shortcuts to an easier time with your infant. So rather than despair at the idea of more tasks, try them and see for yourself which ones help you. Above all, remember that although you are not doing the three phases of *holding time* that you do with an older child, you cannot do too much holding of your newborn. On the contrary, the more you hold your baby, the better your attachment and the happier and easier your baby will be.

7.

THE BOUNCING BABY
AND THE
BELEAGUERED MOTHER

How to Save Energy
While Enjoying Your Crawler

You made it through the first six months, exhausted but on your feet. Your baby seems to sleep a little longer, nurse a little less frequently. You can catch your breath. But just when you have a slight respite, he begins to mobilize. He gets into everything. *Curiosity* is the theme word of the month. He is interested in anything and everything. You have baby-proofed your home, but somehow you know that you must watch him all the time. In any case, he doesn't want to be far away from you or to lose your attention.

Most mothers report that their babies want their attention during this period but don't want to be held for long. Rather the child squirms to climb down. Mothers usually put children down, thinking that it is best to let them explore. But studies of the neurobiology of attachment and separation in primates show how important it is for mother and baby to connect well before and after the baby goes exploring. One type of brain chemical relieves feelings of separation, while another one leads to exploratory behavior. These findings suggest that the young alternately stimulate the two systems by switching between physical contact with the mother and independent play and exploration. Mothers who are not responsive to the amount of alternation needed for maintaining the optimal level of arousal can cause a child to be in a constant state of hyperarousal. Too much arousal is believed to have long-term negative effects on the child's ability to regulate strong emotions.

Marilee was just such a mother. Happily married for four years to a wonderfully loving and demonstrative man, she was now the mother of a beautiful eight-month-old boy, Nicholas. However, both she and her husband were thoroughly exhausted from the demands of this child. He would not sit in his car seat for more than a few minutes without fussing to be picked up. He was already beginning to walk and practiced endlessly. But if Marilee turned her back for a few seconds, he cried to be picked up by her. Neither his baby-sitter nor his grandmother would do. But when Marilee picked him up, he immediately fussed to get down again. Everyone was worn out from trying to keep him happy. He went through this cycle of fussing to be picked up, being picked up by Mommy, then fussing to be put down. When this situation was closely scrutinized, it appeared that the only time he was not fussing was when he was being actively distracted by an adult. Even helping him to fall asleep when he was dog-tired was a chore. He seemed so interested in what was going on around him.

As it turned out, Marilee had been leaving Nicholas with the baby-sitter two or three days a week for at least five hours at a stretch without successfully reconnecting when she came back.

His hyperactivity was most probably a reaction to the separation. As I mentioned earlier, studies have demonstrated that
infants may begin to withdraw after only one hour of separation
from the mother. In any case, *holding* had a calming effect on
this overactive baby. But what a struggle he gave Marilee before
reaching a resolution. He cried and screamed until he turned
purple. Marilee said that for the first time she understood the
expression "purple with rage."

Marilee asked me if an infant saves up his frustrations and
anger the way older children do. I can only infer from an eight-
month-old's behavior, but my guess is that Marilee's baby had
learned to keep his distance in order to protect himself from the
intense feelings he had when his mother was not around. Being
back with his mother didn't calm him easily because it only
reminded him of his anger over prior absences. With older children we have noticed that the cuddling they do after a separation soon gives way to angry rejection of the mother if the
separation lasted longer than their tolerance permitted. Children have even said very directly, "Where have you been when
I wanted you?" Similarly with adults, as much as one wants to
be held by the other, sometimes the hug brings on an angry
outburst. This phenomenon may explain why some people often
ruin a pleasant moment between themselves and a loved one.
Finally achieving the contact they were missing revives their
upset feelings about having missed it.

When Marilee is about to leave Nicholas, he cries as if he will
never see her again. He stops as soon as she picks him up, but
then immediately struggles to climb down, seemingly to avoid
confronting those distressing emotions. In the meantime, he is
not making effective contact with her. If he allowed himself to
feel safe in her arms, his pent-up feelings could burst out. That
is in fact what happened when she picked him up for *holding*
after one of his moments of panic about her impending departure. He cried, screamed, struggled, and then finally relaxed
enough to go to sleep. Marilee thought that he had fallen asleep

out of simple exhaustion. However, he awoke happy and calmly watched her go off to the supermarket without a peep. Marilee's willingness to let him express his rage in the safety of her arms made him feel secure enough to let her go. (See pages 110–115.)

Holding time proved to be a great help for Marilee. But what about her husband? As far as he was concerned, he had a happy, healthy son who didn't need any help. He was annoyed at first that Marilee was using a tool he didn't understand or agree with. But after Marilee explained that it would help the baby feel more secure and be more relaxed, he became interested in the process. Suddenly he realized for himself that their baby had been acting frantic and frustrated. When he saw how happy and calm the baby was afterward, he was convinced that they should use holding regularly.

Marilee's other hurdle was the care-giver. When told about this new method, she was unconvinced. The first two times she heard Nicholas crying, she came running to see what the matter was. But after seeing the positive effects on the baby for herself, she became enthusiastic.

Marilee's baby was overly active, anxious, and easily frustrated. However, the other extreme is just as worrisome. A placid, undemanding baby, usually called "a good baby," can be in similar trouble. Such babies have not become fully engaged in life. When a baby feels secure, his energy is available for exploring the world. If a baby is not eager to explore, we must ask what the baby is doing with his energy.

Obvious examples of such children can be seen with their nannies in New York City's Central Park. The children often sit passively in their strollers without making a peep. I have seen some of the same children act very differently when they are with their mothers, because they feel secure and can free their energy for exploration. I suggest that the rest of the time their energy is diverted into managing the separation from their mothers.

When Holly was nine months old, she was adorable, very

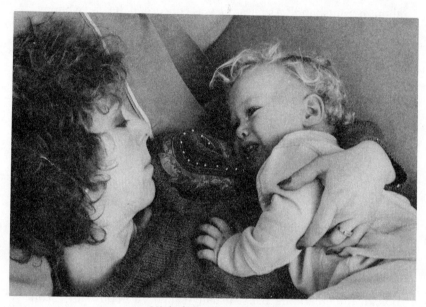

Nicholas cries and cries.

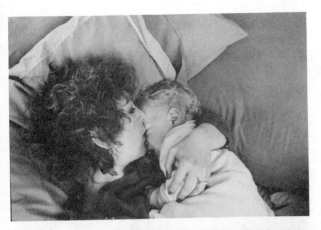

Mother holds on.

Nicholas refuses eye contact and cries hard.

He begins to calm.

*Nicholas snuggles
but still avoids
eye contact.*

He falls alseep.

112

*As he wakes up, he hesitates
between cuddling and escaping.*

He chooses contact.

*He explores
his mother's
face gently.*

*He takes
interest in
her eyes.*

*They begin
a phase of
mutual snuggling.*

Both are joyful.

alert, and interested in her world. She was also very sociable. Anyone who gurgled at her got a happy smile and some vocalizations from her. However, she never protested. She was willing to lie in her crib or sit in the playpen for long periods. By age two and a half, Holly was behind in development. Her speech was not at the expected level for her age, and she was not trying to engage in any activities typical of her agemates. Once *holding time* was initiated, she began to speak above age level and demonstrated exceptional intelligence and competence within a few months, too short a time to attribute her progress to anything other than the secure attachment afforded by her mother through *holding.*

Holding can help the undemanding child whose lack of demands keeps him from having all his needs met. I am not implying that without *holding* all such babies will necessarily have problems later on. Often an overactive baby calms down and a passive baby gets engaged. But now that we know what constitutes optimal development, let's ensure that our babies have a chance to achieve it. Often parents seeking advice for a disturbed child report in retrospect that their child did show signs of insecure attachment at an earlier time.

Any child may exhibit to some degree one or more of these signs at some point, especially when physically ill. However, their presence can represent a warning that there are unmet needs that could quickly be addressed by this method. What follows is a list of some of the symptoms of insecure attachment.

lack of molding to the mother's body when held

frequent squirming to climb down as soon as the child is picked up

frequent avoidance of eye contact

contentment when left alone in the crib or playpen for long periods clinging to rigid routines

strong reactions to small changes

cessation or slowed development of speech

unresponsiveness to soothing or comforting

excessive crying or fussing

teeth grinding

some sleep disturbances

some eating disturbances

destructive behavior, including frequent accidents or injuries

Raymond had walked well since eight months of age. But at twelve months he began to injure himself on furniture or other objects. It seemed as though he always had a bruise or a cut on his face. Christopher also walked at eight months, but at twelve months he had not had so much as a bump. Was Christopher just better coordinated? In the first twelve months of Christopher's life, he was almost always with his mother, often with both mother and father. They were extremely attached to Christopher and interested in his every move. Raymond's mother had been distracted by the family project of remodeling their house. Despite the fact that she usually kept Raymond with her, the amount of intense interaction between them was limited to a few minutes a day. After *holding time* was incorporated into their daily lives, she still worked on the house but was able to stay in better contact with Raymond. She found that not only was the daily session a source of closeness, but she could connect with him in little ways throughout the day much better than before and, significantly, Raymond stopped falling.

Raymond's and Christopher's early experiences bring to mind a study of a tribe in Papua, New Guinea. Before civilization changed their ways, native children were carried on their mothers' bodies for most of the first two years and on someone's body for all of four years. These babies enjoyed secure attachment. They were allowed to play around open fires and sharp knives but were never injured. Accidents just didn't occur. The researchers were also impressed by the combination of character traits exhibited by the adults. They appeared to be self-confident individuals who were also very altruistic. Perhaps we can learn something about how to raise successful children who love others from these "primitive" people.

Thus far we have largely talked about the needs of babies. We must not forget that *holding time* is equally helpful for mothers. You might react to this notion with surprise: "Is it possible for a mother to need this?" Yes, some mothers have found *holding time* helpful for themselves even if everything seems to be going well with the baby. Sometimes you may feel trapped by the demands of a crawling baby. The baby has already required so much care for so many months. If you work, then you are trying to compensate for the hours away by really being there for your baby the rest of the time. Even if you don't work, you may be overwhelmed by the constant vigilance that goes with this particular age.

External pressures may play a significant role. You may find yourself short-tempered or overreacting to your child's minor misbehavior because you are stressed by other issues. *Holding* can help defuse your anger. Occasionally, mothers can feel hurt or rejected by their babies who don't respond in the way, or as much as, they expected. Finally, some mothers may have become depressed from the postpartum hormonal shift and not yet have emerged from the depression.

Whichever is your situation, *holding time* will help you feel better about yourself, your child, your life. When a mother has a very strong bond with a child, she gets rewarded with extra amounts of physical affection, happy vocal responses, an engaging playfulness, and an absence of negative behavior that makes life much more enjoyable.

Darlene is a good example of a mother who needed *holding time* herself. Depression after the birth of her second child was aggravated by the fact that she had not been prepared for another pregnancy. And after her second daughter was born, her first child, a very bright but very demanding girl, became even more demanding. Darlene thought it was lucky that she now had an undemanding, "good baby." However, the good baby failed to develop normally, becoming exceptionally passive and unresponsive. After some months of *holding time,* the first child became easier to manage and the baby came to life as an affectionate, active toddler. Although Darlene has still not fully recovered from depression, she delights in her girls and is gratified by her sense of connection with them.

Lee was worried about herself because she had chosen to continue her career after her baby was born. She felt torn. Her six-month-old baby was an exciting, engaging, adorable little girl, and Lee knew that she would miss her and miss out on watching a wondrous time of development. Although she had hired a warm, expressive, child-loving care-giver for Susie, she knew that it wouldn't be the same as staying home herself. On the other hand, she knew that she would feel trapped and deprived if she didn't continue her career. When Lee heard of *holding time,* she decided to return to work and see if using it could help her to maintain her strong bond with Susie in spite of a daily absence. Lee was shocked to see the rage that Susie expressed during the session each day when she returned home from work. But afterward, the evening was bliss, with Susie affectionate, playful, and happy. On the occasions when she didn't have *holding,* Susie was likely to be cranky, demanding, and rejecting. The difference was so marked that Lee's husband pleaded with her to practice *holding* every day. Lee too was convinced of its usefulness and tried hard to do it every day.

Lee's best friend, Ellen, had heard about this method at the same time. She had been facing the same self-questioning about going to work. She had stayed home for six months after her son's birth. Then she had returned to full-time work. Two years later she gave birth to a daughter but did not stop working. She told Lee that there was a huge difference in her experience with and feeling for her two children. Then her husband's corporate move landed her in a new town with no job. She had to decide whether to take advantage of this natural break to stay home or to find a job once again. Like Lee, Ellen was afraid of feeling trapped, deprived, and maybe even depressed. The two children squabbled a great deal, often making her want to leave for work. She decided to try *holding time* to see if she could tolerate staying home. Within two months, the home environment had changed dramatically. There was almost no vestige of sibling rivalry. While Ellen held one child, the other would either sit at her feet waiting for his or her turn or play independently while she completed the other's *holding* session. This was a big surprise to Ellen because they had been very competitive and impatient before. She had felt that she never had a minute to herself because of their constant demands and especially their competitiveness. If one received even a crumb of special attention, the other wanted an equal share. She rarely even had a chance to go to the bathroom alone. She had forgotten about reading a book or taking a peaceful bubble bath.

One day Ellen realized that she had completely finished preparing dinner without any interruptions from the children. She rushed to see what had happened to them. When she found them happily playing together, she consciously realized that the children had gradually become less and less of a burden. By the third month after starting *holding time,* she felt a marked difference in what she was receiving from the children. Not only had most, if not all, of their negative behavior ceased, but they were giving her more fulfillment and pleasure than she had ever imagined possible. Although she did miss the intellectual challenge of her job, she felt that she was obtaining an emotional fulfillment that equaled the job's challenge. Also, now that she was seeing child development in its most positive form, she was finding it intellectually stimulating as well as emotionally gratifying. She did not feel trapped or depressed. She said she was happier than she had ever been in her life. Further, she felt sure that when she returned to work, she would be able to maintain the same kind of strong attachment with both children that she had achieved with *holding time.* Now that she knew how their relationships could be, she felt she would not have difficulty repairing any disruptions that might occur.

Another factor was the change this more secure mother-child attachment had brought about in Ellen's husband. He came home from work earlier than he ever had before. He loved to be part of the happy scene. He admitted to Ellen that he used to dread coming home to a frazzled wife and two cranky children.

Holding time helped Lee and Ellen in very different ways. It helped Lee go back to work without losing a good connection with her baby, while it enabled Ellen to stay home.

It is a good idea to begin *holding* in the first years of life. But how do you hold a baby who can't talk to you? Is it good to *make* the baby angry? How do you know it is helping your relationship? Once you begin practicing *holding time,* you will see in your baby's behavior an improvement in your attachment. Your baby will mold to your body in the most comfortable cuddling you have ever felt. Your baby will gaze into your eyes more than ever before. Your baby will be calmer yet more alert. Your baby will go to sleep more easily. Your baby will cry less, fuss less, and be frustrated less.

You will not be *making* your baby angry. You will be allowing your baby to express anger in order to become better attached. He can only fully express positive feelings when he is free to express his negative ones as well. Imagine a tribe in which babies refused to be held on the mother's body. They would not survive. Our species would not have survived if mothers and babies had not succeeded in maintaining intimate attachment until the children could really fend for themselves in a hostile environment.

You might wonder how to hold a baby who can't talk. You

pick up the baby in your arms and cuddle him. If he arches his back, averts his gaze, or squirms to be put down, tighten your grasp. He will fight you. You must resolve not to let go until he relaxes happily in your arms. He will most likely become very frustrated. He may cry and scream. Most babies turn pink or purple from intense crying. You may say soothing things to him like, "Momma loves you. I love you." Or you could say, "It hurts my feelings when you don't want me to hold you. I want to be close with you." It is important to speak to your baby. He is studying your language use. But if you don't want to talk some of the time, don't. Just hold. After a while, he will stop fighting you. He will relax. Some babies fall asleep, especially if they are tired because they were too anxious to sleep when they needed to. If possible, hold the baby until he awakens. If he wakes up happy, cooing to you, snuggling into your body, you will know that you had, in fact, reached the resolution phase.

If he awakens still fighting, then you must hold on until he feels better. He is having the equivalent of a tantrum. If you hold him securely, he will calm down and begin to relate to you. If he has a tantrum spontaneously, *holding* is the most effective way of handling his frustration and yours at the same time. Punishing him for having a tantrum communicates that he shouldn't express his feelings. Holding him at that time allows the feelings to be expressed in a way that avoids creating more problems; in the future, *holding* will defuse the feelings before they reach an explosive tantrum level.

I will never forget the first resolution I saw with one eight-month-old. His *holding* was filmed on videotape by a colleague. The baby struggled fiercely and then after about forty minutes melted into his mother's chest. Yes, forty minutes! He gazed into her eyes with a beatific smile on his face and gurgled at her. Then he stroked her face gently with his chubby little hand. Cindy, his mother, had started *holding time* with another child, a daughter, because of her behavior problems. The father, too, participated with each child and with Cindy. When I met them several months after they had been doing this regularly, they were the very picture of an ideal family.

Please remember that all mothers feel very upset, if not pained, by the fight that their babies give them when they first start. It is truly shocking to see how much resistance your baby has. You must persevere. Just remember that all children reach a resolution if their mothers hold on long enough. And try to imagine during the struggle how happy you will be to see your baby completely relaxed and totally connected to you when you reach a resolution. Once you have been through a whole cycle, through the rejection phase and on to a resolution, you will never again be afraid of your baby's anger. You will never again be at a loss when your child has a tantrum. The most important thing you can do during a tantrum is to hold your child tightly and safely in your arms until he recovers and can relate happily once again.

One day when our children were babies, my good friend Judith and I took them into Central Park. Because her daughter had a tantrum, Judith sat down on a park bench and initiated *holding* right there. I was embarrassed to see a policeman coming along the path. I moved away from my friend, as if to say, "I'm not with them. Isn't that terrible?" As if in reply, the policeman smiled and said, "It looks pretty loving to me." Then I was really ashamed. I had practically renounced my own method. I have tears in my eyes just thinking about it. Certainly you won't always have the understanding of strangers if you do it in public, but other mothers have reported receiving positive support. And of course they are doubly rewarded, because the child's behavior shapes up immediately.

Occasionally some mothers have more difficulty tolerating the resolution than the rejection phase. The degree of intimacy achieved in the resolution phase is a new experience for them. If this happens to you, then you must recognize that to enjoy experiencing intimacy may require some adjustments on your part. Force yourself at first. You will come to revel in it. Don't allow yourself to interrupt it by stopping too soon. Allow yourself and your baby the warmth, tenderness, and closeness of those incomparable moments. It is my belief that many mothers and fathers who never enjoyed true intimacy with their own parents learn intimacy from their children. This phenomenon may explain why some older couples I have met seem to reach a deep level of intimacy with each other only later in life, after they have enjoyed some years of intimacy with their children.

Some mothers have difficulty with one phase and not the others. Some mothers have difficulty with all the phases at first. Some mothers take to *holding time* as if they have always been doing it. The major determining factor seems to be their own parents' relationship with them when they were children. So if you are one of the lucky ones, you will find the process easy. If not, you will have to work a little harder. In any case, all mothers can learn to use *holding time.* You can too.

8.

THE TANTRUM-PRONE TODDLER AND THE FRAZZLED MOTHER

How to Avoid the Terrible Twos

In the second year most mothers have a hard time no matter how well behaved their toddler is. At this age the child is in perpetual motion, and the mother may find herself depleted and exhausted.

The toddler is very curious, very mobile, yet very dependent on the mother's presence and uninterrupted attention. If she does follow her child around attentively while he explores the world, she will have a relatively happy child whose physical and intellectual growth is optimally stimulated. However, she will usually feel drained and somewhat stupefied. How many times have you heard a toddler's mother say that she is no longer fit to engage in adult conversation? This feeling is a direct result of our way of raising children today. We were meant to rear children in large family groups with other mothers and many children, including a full range of ages. In fact, animal behaviorists have discovered that the great apes cannot raise their young in isolation without becoming abusive or neglectful. When they are in groups with other mothers, the very same mothers who when alone appeared disturbed and dangerous become good mothers.

In essence, we are asking mothers to raise children in a setting that is not supportive of good mothering. Our answer has been to put the children into groups such as day care or nursery school. We need groups for mothers and children together. City parks simulate such a setting. Many community centers offer mother-child groups. La Leche is another group that brings mother and child together with other mothers and children.

There is, however, a danger in joining groups. Many mothers are so starved for adult contact that they fail to pay attention to their children during the group activity. *Holding time* helps a mother and child to focus on each other, to express their needs clearly, and to be attuned to each other no matter what the setting. A mother can learn to make contact with adults and at the same time pay attention to her child. She responds to her toddler's constant need to touch base and then go exploring. She is not impatient with his demands. She understands that his need for her attention is real and not manipulative. She is not embarrassed when he interrupts her conversation. She learns to put aside her embarrassment in the interests of her toddler's development. She chooses settings that are supportive of her paying attention to him.

If you work and leave your child with a care-giver, remember that all the statements about mothers' needing a supportive setting apply as well to your child's care-giver. This is why you see nannies clustering together daily in New York's Central Park. If you leave a care-giver at home in isolation with your child, you are more apt to have a depressed care-giver. If you do not live near a park where babies spend time, try to send your toddler and care-giver to a community center regularly. Or at least send them out to lunch or to a shopping mall or someplace where people might speak to them. However, they should not spend all their time away from home, since home offers the security of the familiar when you are gone. Your child may also feel better being home around the time when you usually return, because then he doesn't fear that he will miss your homecoming. But some time out with others can be helpful to both your child and the care-giver.

While I was training in child psychiatry, I took care of a friend's two children in their home while she was away for two weeks. The four-year-old refused to go to nursery school. When I told my supervisor about this dilemma, she advised me to make a calendar showing when Mommy would come home. The next day the child went off to nursery school without a moment's hesitation and told the teacher, "Mommy will not come home today." As soon as she knew that she would not miss Mommy's homecoming, she felt able to go.

A problem for many parents is the fact that toddlers want to have control. By now, they have discovered that they can affect things and people by their actions and are enchanted by seeing how much they can do. It is very important that they be allowed to control you and their environment some of the time. Try to plan time when you can follow your child's lead. Allow him to explore whatever interests him and talk about it with him. The greatest learning occurs when a child is highly motivated. If you allow your child free rein, he will be maximally motivated to explore. This will be a time of intense learning behavior. He will develop a sense of his capacity to influence you in a very positive way. This sense is the foundation of self-esteem. If you refuse to allow him this degree of control, he will not feel good about himself, and he might also incessantly try to control inappropriate issues and constantly be at loggerheads with you in the hopes that he will eventually be able to influence you. If he feels totally powerless, he may give up entirely. This situation often leads to overall poor motivation.

When you cannot allow him to do something because it is dangerous or undesirable, firmly tell him he cannot do it. A toddler learns reality from your reactions to his actions. If you say no only when necessary, for instance when he reaches for the hot stove, he learns not to do it. If you allow him free rein to do safe things, when you say a strong no he will believe you. If you say no all the time, then he won't believe you when he wants to touch the hot stove. Not trusting your warning, he will test everything for himself. He will feel unsafe because he has the burden of discovering all reality for himself.

The toddler is a very ambitious creature. He wants to explore everything. He tries to do things beyond his skills. To make matters worse, his expressive language does not measure up to his comprehension level. Therefore, your toddler becomes frustrated often. You have the difficult task of managing his frustration. You need to be very patient, which is especially difficult when you yourself are the object of so many demands.

The remedy for your toddler's frustration and your impatience is *holding time.* If you give your toddler this outlet, you will find that his tolerance for frustration rises dramatically. This automatically eases the strain on your patience. In addition, it raises your tolerance for everything, whether it is the toddler's demands, his frustrations, or the pressures from other aspects of your life. *Holding time* with a toddler brings with it the reward of a very close and deeply gratifying attachment at a point when many mothers and children lose that wonderful connection.

Toddlers are known for tantrums, but "the terrible twos" is not an unavoidable developmental stage. It is not seen in primitive societies where babies are carried on their mothers' bodies.

The pattern of the terrible twos is a symptom of mother-child detachment.

When your toddler has a tantrum, pick him up and begin *holding*. Tell him to *go ahead and get those feelings out*. He will understand you, but he will fight you, he will cry, he will rage, and he may even try to bite you. Do not allow biting or other injury to you, or to him either for that matter. Hold him tightly. Tell him that you will hold him until you both feel better. He may call for Daddy. Listen, but do not act on this request. Do not interrupt the process. He may put up a struggle that will scare and devastate you by its intensity and duration. Just make sure that you hold him until the resolution. You cannot mistake the resolution; the anger and resistance will dissolve into expressions of love and tenderness beyond your expectations.

I will describe to you a typical toddler *holding time*. Betty decided to hold twenty-month-old Amy because she was refusing kisses and eye contact when Betty returned from work. The refusals were extending to other times. When Betty told Amy she was going to hold her, Amy began to cry immediately. She said, "No kisses. Amy doesn't want Mommy kisses." She cried; she pulled away; she refused to look at her mother. Amy mentioned several upsetting events. Betty discussed those events with her and tried to reassure the child. She continued to hold despite Amy's continuing struggle to free herself. Finally Amy looked at Betty, touched her eye, and said, "Hi, eyes. What doing?" Then began a period of intense eye contact and gentle face stroking. Betty asked for a kiss. Amy gave it. Then Amy hugged Betty briefly. Betty asked for more. Amy closely embraced her mother. Then she lay back and looked lovingly at her mother, saying, "Mommy, you beautiful." Betty said, "You are beautiful too." Amy said, "Amy and Mommy, Amy and Daddy beautiful." Then she turned to her daddy and called, "Da, you are beautiful." When he came closer, she said, "I love you too, Da. Amy and Mommy, Amy and Daddy beautiful." This resolution brought such happiness to this family that the father became an avid proponent of *holding time* and began to fully participate in the process by often holding his wife during her *holding time* with Amy.

Another example of toddler *holding time* is the case of Alexander, thirteen months old. He was a well-developed, even precocious, bouncing baby who walked at eight months. He was happy, energetic, and easy to comfort. Then the family went on vacation. In a strange place, he seemed to need more holding, more reassurance, and less physical distance when he explored. By the end of the first week of the vacation, Kelly, his mother, was slightly stir-crazy. Having learned about *holding time* from a friend, she decided to use it in hopes of salvaging the vacation. The result was that Kelly found Alexander needed less reassurance than ever before. He became more of a cuddler when he came back to her for refueling of affection. In other words, he was able to make more effective use of her affection and comforting. Instead of coming back for less than a minute in her arms, he lingered longer but needed it less often. Kelly assumed that he felt more secure when she saw that he expected her to follow him around less and his frustration tolerance improved. For both mother and child, life became easier and more peaceful. Anyone who had known this pair would never have thought that there was any need for improvement. In fact, they did have an excellent bond. However, in the case of healthy mother-child attachment, more is always better.

One thing to keep in mind with your toddler is your own communication. Toddlers understand everything you say. It is a terrible mistake to equate a child's expressive language with what he comprehends. By the time you discover that your toddler was understanding everything, it is too late to take back what you said. Many mothers lower their voices when talking about a topic they don't want to discuss in front of a toddler. Lowering your voice is a red flag to a child, who will automatically prick up his ears. In fact, if you want a child to learn a foreign language, speak it mainly in hushed tones, as if you're trying to hide something from him. Motivation is the greatest enhancer of learning. If you really don't want your child to hear something, do not say it in his presence. However, I recommend a more practical view. Children usually know all that is going on. Rather than try to hide information, be open. Let your toddler deal with reality. His concerns will come up in *holding time,* and you will be able to help him cope with them.

A situation that is easily mishandled is an upcoming change. Parents often wait to tell a child about plans because they anticipate a negative reaction. *Holding* provides a way for parent and child to prepare for the event ahead of time. The distress is confined, and the end result is that the child is prepared to handle the event when it does occur. Of course you cannot anticipate all causes of distress. *Holding* also helps a child deal with an upsetting event after it has occurred.

Annie's family flew on an airplane to visit her grandparents. After they were safely back home, during *holding* Annie revealed her unresolved upset. Her mother helped her to see that her fears of falling were not realized because they had landed softly and safely. Without *holding time,* Annie might have retained a fear of flying without anyone's realizing it.

If your toddler is clingy, demanding, cranky, irritable, rejecting, or hyperactive and overly independent, then you need the enhanced communication and better attachment available through *holding time.* It will help your toddler happily enjoy exploration of his widening world as much as he enjoys cuddling or romping with you.

9.

THE PRECOCIOUS PRESCHOOLER AND THE PRESSURED MOTHER
How to Maximize Your Child's Potential

The preschool-age child can be a delight or a nightmare. The choice is entirely up to you. A child of this age can be great fun and yet in part still be just an affectionate, cuddly baby. By age four, children are able to sustain short separations for the first time without cost to their ability to trust you. The new ability to separate means that they are now really ready to enjoy nursery school or a play group. You can have some free time without jeopardizing their well-being.

They become very interested in roles. They copy everything

they see and act it out in imaginative play. It is the best entertainment possible for a well-bonded mother. Now they are capable of playing with, not just alongside, another person. If you stimulate their imaginations, they can play endlessly either with you or beside you while you do other things; they will still stay in contact by speaking to you all the while or from time to time.

Play is the work of childhood. It is the foundation for all learning and for creative problem-solving. Play should be encouraged. It is best stimulated by parent-child play. How many times were you told to go play as a child? If you don't enjoy play now, you can assume that your parents did not play with you very well or very much. In any case, an important aspect of parenting is playing with your child. If you do not know how or don't like to play, then you can learn now. To some extent you may have to force yourself. The best way to learn is to choose things you most like to do. If you like to paint, play with finger paints. If you like to build, play with blocks. If you like trains, buy a train set.

The hours of play will be a wonderfully rewarding time with your child that you will both always cherish. And your child will learn to value play and be interested in it if you are. Studies have demonstrated that certain kinds of play foster particular skills. For example, playing with blocks lays the foundation for math ability. Traditionally, boys have been better at math than girls have. Ask a girl who is very good at math if she played with blocks. Usually the answer will be yes.

Physical exercise like wrestling, jumping, running, and climbing promotes all development. A study followed two matched groups of preschoolers. One group was given physical exercise mainly involving gross motor activity while the other was given the more traditional small motor activity of a nursery school program. After ten years the exercise group was more outstanding not just in physical prowess but in academics and in leadership. If there is any activity you want your preschooler really to enjoy and pursue, then do it with him. Parents are the most powerful motivators. Your true interest will be communicated by your actual involvement. The majority of great tennis players learned to play with a parent. And when they showed promise, the parent or parents trekked around watching them take lessons or compete. I am not trying to help you make athletes or musicians or any other kind of professionals out of your children. I merely want to tell you that your involvement in your child's play will lead to his increased ability to play, which will in turn lead to better learning. All the while you will be enjoying each other.

Too much organized activity is being thrust upon many preschoolers. Some children go to preschool as well as tumbling classes and ballet and swimming and so on. You can avoid this kind of needless overprogramming of your child by playing with him yourself. Children need uncomplicated time. Their need is not to rush from place to place or activity to activity, but to relax and remain free to explore their own world at their own pace. They do not need much formally arranged peer interaction at this juncture. If it happens naturally, then try to keep it limited. If you work, you may tend to program your child's time so that you won't feel guilty about being absent. You can avoid this mistake by letting your child stay at home with a care-giver. Let them play together. Think of activities that you can set up for them to enjoy together if your care-giver is not a natural player. There are children's magazines that suggest good activities. And make sure they go outdoors every day for large-muscle activity.

If your child is overprogrammed, one unfortunate consequence will be that he must thereafter always be kept busy and entertained, never learning to relax and enjoy free time. If your child goes to a play group or nursery school, then the rest of his time is better spent on less programmed activities.

Children can enjoy some peer play at this stage. However, most children are being pushed into it too much. If you want your child to be able to resist peer pressure later, do not push him now. If you push, you will be giving him the message that you think peers are very important. It will be difficult, if not impossible, to retract that message later in the teens when overinvolvement with peers can be really dangerous. The best message you can give your child is, "I love you. I want you home with the family. Let's be with each other." If you give this message, you will have a child with good self-esteem who will have no problem with peers either in the present or in the future.

Often children are pushed into actions they are not ready for by adults trying to help them be sociable. How often we hear parents tell a child, "Say hello to Mrs. Smith." The best way to teach a child to be sociable is by example. If you are sociable and your child is not, then something is wrong. Try not to force an unnatural action. Forcing just makes it worse anyway, because you lower your child's self-esteem. Instead, try to help the child to want to do it himself. Prepare your child to respond ahead of time: "We are going to the party now. Mrs. Smith has worked hard to make it nice for us. What could you say to her to let her know we appreciate her invitation?" Then let your child decide what to say. If he doesn't want to say anything, ask him what he wants you to say for him. *Holding time* is a good opportunity to discuss social interactions with others. Because you are most tuned in to each other's feelings during this period, this is the easiest time to help your child empathize with other people. Then, too, because you are raising the issue, he will realize how important it is to you. His wanting to please you will help to motivate him.

Sometimes parents ask a child to do some necessary task and then insist that he *want* to do it too. At this stage be glad that your preschooler normally wants to do what you want. He is incorporating your values if he is in good connection with you. Even in adult life it is not always reasonable to expect another person to do what you want and to want it as well. His doing it for you is better than good enough.

Holding time leads to sociability because it helps the child to be self-confident and attuned to others' feelings. If you have been giving your child the kind of love and attention we have been discussing, then you probably have an exceptional child who surprises you with his or her apparent precocity. This good development can be supported by using *holding*.

Preschool age is a very important period for *holding time* because of the child's increasing ability to separate from you. Many mothers sense this new ability and let go of their children too completely. When you let go at this stage, you often don't realize the consequences until months or years later. It takes time for the destructive effects of too little togetherness to wear down the strength built up by good early years. It is similar to tooth decay: an abscess takes a long time to develop from a tiny cavity in good enamel. Holding will strengthen your child's ability to separate. When you have a very good bond, the child is free to go off comfortably, knowing he can come back any time and be close with you. Your child learns that *freedom to separate is not gained at the expense of intimacy*. This lesson is one of the most important for present as well as future relationships, especially in marriage.

Another major benefit of *holding time* for this age group is the continuous buildup of self-esteem and feelings of being acceptable and accepted. Your child's feelings, which he equates with his very self, must be OK if he can express them to his mother and she accepts them.

Holding time helps a preschooler to increase his verbal facility. It turns out that allowing a free flow of feelings leads to very complete verbal expression of those feelings. There appears to be a correlation between the ability to express feelings and the development of a generally advanced use of language, because *holding time* has helped speech-delayed preschoolers.

The very best result of using this approach is the mutual closeness that can be achieved. The preschool years can be a wonderful period in your life because your child is still very much your little girl or boy. Children this age are not yet off into the mastery phase of the primary grade youngster. They really are not as interested in peers as they will be later. Although the older child will also be capable of great closeness, the preschooler combines the verbal ability to express a great deal of feeling with the propensity to remain with you in a way that the demands of later development will preclude. Your chief aim with the preschooler is to help him maximize his potential while he can still be with you in a major way. Traditional books on child development list the milestones—such as smiling, opening of the hands, obvious recognition of the mother, as well as problem-solving and language comprehension—as coming much later in development than is observed in children who are raised with intense mother-child contact. If you are not satisfied with the present intensity of your contact, you can compensate now with daily *holding.* Children who appear to be exceptional by school age have had the kind of contact discussed in the chapters on the earlier phases. As babies they had a great deal of togetherness, being carried on their mothers' bodies, being nursed by their mothers, sleeping with their mothers and fathers at least in the early months, being talked to constantly by their mothers and others, being handled, massaged, caressed, and gazed at by their mothers and fathers. Babies handled in this way on the average develop faster and are happier, more sociable, and easier to comfort and regulate.

Although these children appear to be exceptional at preschool age, it may be that they are merely reaching optimal development earlier. It is very likely that many such children have inherited intelligence, but perhaps a larger percentage of children would be as exceptional if their development was as positively fostered. Many professionals believe that certain personality traits are inborn. However, further examination of the effect of very early handling on newborns suggests that the type of handling is the most important determining factor and that the environment can enhance or diminish or negate the effects of inborn characteristics.

A mother named Sally gave me insight into the importance of early handling. She brought her fourth child to me when Sue was six months old. The family was "complete": two boys, two girls, just what they wanted. The timing of the pregnancy had been exactly as they had planned. So why, she asked, was her baby so impossible? Sue was irritable and rejected human contact. Even while she nursed, she pushed her mother away with one hand. She refused to make eye contact and would only allow herself to be carried if she was sucking on her pacifier. Sally claimed to have treated Sue the same as the other three children. On further questioning, Sally revealed that she had fretted during the whole pregnancy because she really didn't want to be tied down once again, and she was certain that her fourth child couldn't be as terrific as the other three because no mother could be so lucky. She recalled her negative feelings during labor and at the moment of birth. She remembered that Sue had been a calm, easy baby for two weeks before becoming irritable. She did not start rejecting Sally until a few weeks later. Three months of *holding time* helped Sally establish a strong attachment with this baby. Now Sally says Sue is her most affectionate and her most accomplished child. By preschool age, she was a computer whiz as well as an exceptionally capable athlete.

Sally thinks, in looking back, that Sue was in fact no different from the other three but that her own lack of positive feelings for the baby affected her handling of this child. Once she handled her more like the others, Sue developed comparably. But Sally attributes Sue's greater capacity for affection and closeness and her more outstanding physical and intellectual achievement to *holding time.*

A word about expectations: studies done in grade schools have demonstrated that children who were labeled outstanding became exceptional whether or not they had shown any signs of unusual potential before they were labeled. Conversely, many children with exceptional intelligence do not develop to their potential because of either emotional problems or low expectations from their family or teachers. *Holding* helps a mother to have high expectations because she becomes better attuned to her child, which means she knows more precisely what he is capable of. She also feels that she is giving him her very best, so she expects him to do the same. Knowing what a child is capable of and asking for it, in combination with giving a child the love, care, and attention he needs, is the basic formula for successful child rearing. Often parents expect too much or too little because they do not understand what the child's capabilities are. Sometimes parents have expectations which the child cannot meet, not because he is not capable at that level, but because he is not receiving the support and nurturing he needs to behave up to par.

At this stage of development, how parents order their priorities begins to be especially important, though this is important no matter what the age of the child. My priority principle is that you weigh your actions according to the message they convey about your values. If a child spills his milk on the rug, be careful not to make him feel that the rug is more important than he is. If your child disturbs your pancake making, remember that your goal is a nurturing breakfast experience. Eating together happily is more important than pancakes.

If you always ask yourself what is most important, you will usually act according to your priorities. If you act automatically, you will often put something unimportant in first place because of the heat of the moment. If you keep in mind that you are trying to maintain a strong attachment, the way you handle your child's mishaps will be better for you both. If you think the mishaps are deliberate, do *holding*. If they are, then that will come out during your session and be resolved. If the mishap was not intentional, that also will become apparent. You will then feel like apologizing. No harm will have been done by extra holding. In fact, it will be a preventive action. You will be all the closer for having done it.

If you practice regular *holding time* with your preschooler, you will have a child who is free to maximize his potential so that when he goes off to grade school he is more likely to be full of confidence, curiosity, and motivation, with a great capacity for relating well to other people.

10.

THE ENTERPRISING YOUNGSTER AND THE SIDELINED MOTHER

How You and Your Husband Can Support Your Child's Optimal Development

When a child reaches first grade, many changes become apparent. Most children are ready for a structured learning situation by this time. They stay in school for a full day. They begin to form real friendships of their own choice, not just those occasioned by proximity or by parental direction. They begin to be more reactive to peers as a group. They begin to be interested in mastery of all kinds: sports, carpentry, mechanics, sewing, cooking, and any skills they see in older siblings or their parents. They begin to push for more independence.

If children are going to achieve optimal development at this juncture, they need a tremendous amount of backing in the form of parental attention, love, and nurturing. Yet it is just at this point that the majority of mothers who have maintained a good connection up until now begin to let go of their children too much. Because the child seems competent and because the child is occupied in constructive pursuits, the mother mistakenly steps back. Some mothers are so burdened that they are relieved to have a child more or less able to be left on his own. They inadvertently allow the child to slip away. It may be a long time, maybe even a few years, before they realize that something has happened to their relationship.

This situation will never develop with you and your child if you practice *holding*. You will find that your child does go off on his ventures toward mastery, but you will always have a way of restoring your connection. If anything, your child will be more independent than before. But he will not be slipping away. He will freely return to you for nurturing and to give love to you. He will not just do this when he feels like it. He will do it when he feels like it *and* when he sees you need it, as well as when you ask for it. So often mothers say that there is no problem because their children do hug them. But in reality the children do it only on their own terms, not in a mutual way. The mother is forced to wait for the child to feel like hugging. You do your child no favor when you allow this kind of one-sided relationship. A great gift you can give your children is the capacity to give of themselves when others need it or want it, not just when it is something they do for themselves. The pattern you two establish will be the model for his other relationships. *Holding time* ensures a child's capacity to create a mutually gratifying relationship. Grab your child now before any more development time passes. Hold on until you feel the mutual exchange of affection, tenderness, love, and open communication.

Some mothers feel genuinely sad when their children reach the mastery stage. A mother often longs for the times when a chubby baby was happy to lie in her arms, to sit on her lap, and to give her sloppy, wet kisses. In fact, such feelings of longing often lead to another pregnancy. Mothers feel that they are supposed to let go and allow their children to separate, to grow up, to move on to other people and activities. Our culture has taught them to feel guilty if they don't let go. If you feel this way, you have let go too much. Mothers with good attachment develop a gauge for sensing what is right. The trouble is that we have been indoctrinated to think these feelings are a sign of a mother's problems. This is not true. Trust your feelings. Your and your child's feelings are the best indicators of how the relationship should be. If you are sad about losing your growing child, then you are not maintaining adequate attachment. When you have good attachment you feel very satisfied and even joyous about your relationship. Anytime you find yourself not feeling joyous, try holding. Tell your child that you want to be close. Tell him that the busy pace of your lives is standing in the way of your good feelings for each other, that even though the good feelings are there, they are not expressed and enjoyed by the two of you as much as you would like. Remember how you felt when he was a cuddly baby? You will feel that warm, happy feeling after *holding* a child of any age.

If you are an overprotective mother, you need *holding time* even more. Don't let anyone tell you that you need to separate from your child. What you need is a better connection. You can change the overprotectiveness into a more balanced relationship in which you both survive the separations and remain close without clinging.

Let's see what might be happening between you and your child at this stage. Does your child withdraw from you? If so, your natural reaction will be to pull him back. You fall into a vicious cycle where your attempts to keep him close make him withdraw more. You probably wind up angry with each other often. You may feel very unappreciated. He may feel very constrained. He may think that you don't have confidence in him.

In any case, the two of you are not enjoying a reciprocity of feelings. *Holding time* can repair this situation in short order. Each time you have a holding session, you will find out how your child feels about your overprotective pull. You may find out that he feels the need to compensate for your pull by going farther than even he feels comfortable going. You may find that he feels that he can't trust your judgment about what he can do because you are always pulling him back, whether the given situation calls for it or not. He may tell you that he has to search for the limits of what he can do because he cannot use you as a guide.

When you hear such feelings and thoughts from your child, you will have insight that will help you to respond more appropriately. When you tell him your feelings that have led to your overprotectiveness, he will understand why you act the way you do. The empathy he feels for you will help him stop being angry and rejecting. You may be giving the message that you don't appreciate the things he is competent to do, and this can lead him to go too far in trying to prove himself. But if he understands the source of your feelings and feels closer to you because of it, then he is likely to assuage your worries *in advance*. It will help you both to talk. Children are definitely capable of discussions. But *holding time* does more: it connects feelings and thoughts in a way that simple discussion does not. Better understanding can be reached with both the feelings and thoughts in perspective.

Holding time is also useful with a clinging, shy, fearful, or babyish child. People often think that such children need a boost toward independence. If your child is talking baby talk, he is signaling you that he needs babying. This is the time to fill his need. After the rejection phase, play baby with him. Talk baby talk to him. Cuddle him like a baby. Tell him you will baby him as much as he wants during this special contact, but the rest of the time you want him to behave normally. Once you have given him this message, you are obliged to follow through on it. He will continue to ask to be babied, but he will confine the baby play to *holding time*. As you begin to satisfy his need, he will ask to be babied less and less. Once he discovers that he can have his needs for nurturing met on his age-appropriate level, he will begin to prefer behaving appropriately.

A shy child is in the same boat with the passive baby discussed in Chapter 7. This child is so busy worrying about his security that he does not have the energy to meet the world head-on and explore its possibilities. If you have a child who seems a little shy in certain situations, the discussions you prompt during *holding* will reveal his source of insecurity, and you will be able to help him understand himself. Furthermore, the very process will give him greater security through better attachment and communication with you. He will not feel so alone and defenseless. Some people might say, "Why make a fuss about a little shyness? I was shy too." Just because you recovered from shyness does not mean that your child will. In any case, a child need not be left alone to tough it out when there is a better solution. *Holding time* will provide a good enough connection to free your child's energies to confront the world.

Fearfulness is another manifestation of an insecure base. Normal development takes place in a secure context provided by the family group, most directly the mother. If your child is fearful, chances are that your connection with your child is not as good as it needs to be. Many mothers are exasperated by this notion of faulty connection, especially if they are giving a great deal of attention to the child. Remember that what is offered is not always utilized efficiently. It is not enough to give. *What you give has to be received by your child. Holding time* ensures that what you can give is utilized. The very process of *holding* makes it possible for the child to put what the mother offers to good use. The mother becomes a sounding board for the child. She becomes a receptacle for the child's excess baggage of distress, anger, misunderstandings, hurt, and other negative feelings. In accepting the child's feelings, the mother creates an open channel for direct communication. What *holding time* makes possible is a demonstration of unconditional love, the best and most secure base a mother can offer a child.

If your child is clinging, he is giving you a loud message that he does not feel he has enough of you. If you are upset with this idea because you think you give so much time and attention to your growing child, think about how he is experiencing you. Holding will help you gain this kind of empathy. You may give your child a great deal of time. But if he is clinging or even just asking for more, chances are that he is not receiving enough from you. In this case, it is not necessarily more time that he needs. A more direct delivery system is required. Ask your child how he would like to spend time with you if he could choose. He may not really know. There is a good possibility that even when you do find extra time to spend with your child, he does not feel that it is enough. *Holding time* will solve this problem. The contact established in just one session will be much more complete than any activity you have ever done with him before. You will both feel very satisfied.

If your child seems otherwise in a good state but is having some difficulties with school, then you need to hold before school each day. It releases children's energy for learning, for concentrating, for cooperating, and for getting along with other children.

Seven-year-old Jeff and his mother had been doing *holding time* more or less regularly for three years. One day Jeff came home from school in a state of excitement. He wanted his mother to call Eric's mother to tell her about it. Eric was having difficulty sitting still, following directions, and dealing with his peers. Jeff knew from his experience with his mom that holding was helpful to him in these areas. He was excited to think that Eric's problems could be solved if only his mother would do the same. Jeff's mother was pleased to find out that he saw *holding time* as a possible solution to other children's behavior problems.

Sometimes children compare themselves unfavorably with

others. In kindergarten Brian noticed that his classmates could draw much better than he. He and his mother had been using *holding time* occasionally to deal with upsets. During one session he confided to his mother that he rarely attempted drawing because he was not able to draw the way his friend Joy could. Once his upset feelings had been shared with his mother, he felt free to try drawing. Very soon afterward he was creating very complex, imaginative drawings. His actual skill wasn't as great as Joy's at that point in development; however, his rich imagination made up for this lack. He had a good time drawing, liked his work, and received positive feedback from everyone who saw his efforts. His upset had blocked his willingness to try. After *holding,* his energies were free for drawing. His mother felt that this issue might never have come to her attention without the communication engendered by *holding time.*

During *holding,* May finds out many things that have bothered ten-year-old Sammy since age three. She is astonished by his memory for details, including the exact day and date something happened, the year and make of a visitor's car, or his thoughts and feelings from a short interaction that occurred five or six years ago. Although she is upset at hearing some of these memories, they talk about them and most often resolve the issues. She is relieved to know that her son does not have to go through life weighted down by this unpleasant baggage. One day after a resolution, this child said to his mother, "I can't tell you what I am thinking. You won't be able to take it." After some encouragement, he said, "I used to hate you." This statement was an indication of the rage he used to feel when they were poorly connected. She told him she knew and accepted his feelings even though it hurt to hear him say it. He burst out in a very happy smile, hugged her to him, and said, "Mommy, I love you." It was a moment of pure joy for both of them. You too will discover that you can accept all of your child's feelings through *holding time.* When you have achieved this goal, your child will have good self-esteem, which is the basis for a happy,

successful start in the world. In the meantime, you will be enjoying a wonderful, close, warm relationship, which will be a model
for his relationships throughout life.

The father is important at every stage of development, but his
role becomes more complex at school age. First of all, the issues
of size, strength, and prowess become increasingly significant
for the growing child. The father is idealized as the ultimate
power. This idealization makes the child feel protected from the
dangers of the world. Perhaps more important, it serves to protect the child from his own impulses. Limits are very important
to a child's sense of security. Parents who provide a well-delin-
eated structure are perceived as caring. Children give parents
credit for providing such structure, even if they protest that it is
more than they want.

A nurturing, nondictatorial father-protector, who is viewed as
an ultimate but benign authority and who works in concert with
a nurturing mother, is essential to an ideal team for raising
happy and successful children. A harsh or authoritarian father
will produce either a rebellious or an unmotivated child. An
uninvolved father will produce a child with low self-esteem who
is not confident enough to strive.

It is the father's function to encourage the child to try new
skills. Usually fathers have greater success in pushing a child
into action. This may be a result of the child's need for his dad's
approval. How often have you heard a child discount a compli-
ment from his mom because "she is prejudiced"? This is not all
bad. It means the child knows that his mom loves and admires
him. Given this base, a father can encourage him easily because
he wants his father's admiration and praise and because he
already has his mother's approval.

If you are interested in your child's mastery of some particular
skill, have your husband work on it with him too. For example,
both parents should read to a child, and both parents should

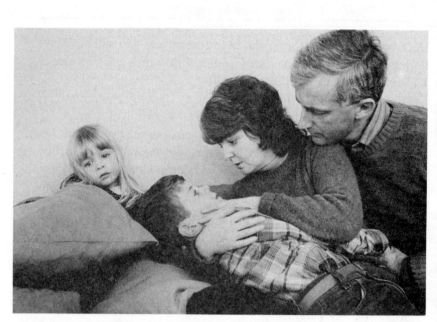

John does not physically resist holding.

Instead he tells his mom he doesn't want to hold.

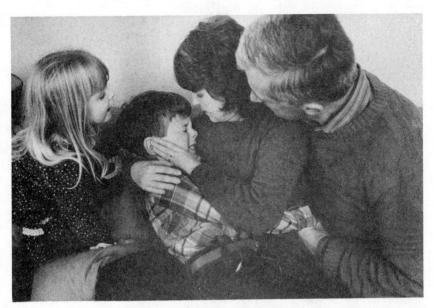

John cries as he gets in touch with his feelings.

He yells.

*They struggle
for what seems
an eternity.*

*John begins
to calm down.*

150

*He looks into
his mother's eyes
but remains upset.*

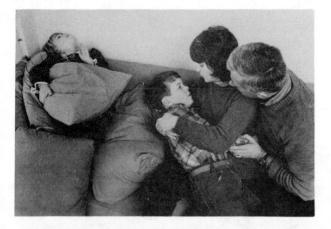

Now he willingly looks at his mom and begins to talk.

After twenty minutes of sharing feelings, he turns to kiss Sarah.

He kisses Mom some more.

He hugs Dad.

He hugs Sarah.

have the child read to them. The same is true for any other skill. In addition, time spent together using skills the child is ready to start learning, from reading to hammering to playing ball, can inspire the child to make use of the father's involvement and encouragement so that they both enjoy his newfound progress. This shared time can be the foundation for having the child incorporate the joy of learning into his own value system.

The most important role of the father is to love the mother and child and to show it clearly in time spent with them and in physical demonstrations of affection. Before urbanization, the extended family provided support and contact for a mother and child. Now the nuclear family must provide all that for itself. Therefore, it is really imperative for a mother and father to establish a mutually gratifying relationship that will allow them to support each other in providing a good environment for the growing child.

School age is the time when the majority of mothers inadvertently allow a premature break in strong attachment because the child is oriented toward independence and mastery. If children are going to achieve optimal development throughout the rest of their lives, they need a tremendous amount of support at this stage in the form of parental attention, love, and nurturing. If your child resists your nurturing, then you must break through his resistance. Not providing adequate parenting at this stage could have serious repercussions during the teen years. The goal of *holding time* is to allow your child his independence while at the same time ensuring a deep and effective ongoing connection.

PART THREE

Holding Time in Special Situations

11.

THE WORKING MOTHER
AND THE
SELF-RELIANT CHILD

How You Can Maintain a Good
Relationship
with Your Child and Keep Working

Today most American mothers go off to work while their children are still preschoolers. The reality is that only about 12 percent of women stay at home full-time. If you are like most working mothers, you probably can't help wondering if your absence is bad for your child. No matter how fulfilled a mother is by her career or how much she needs her job to support the family, she may often worry that she could be sacrificing her child's well-being because she divides her time and energy between work and family. This is a valid concern, but worrying won't help. *Holding time* will.

Throughout history mothers have worked. Farm women have always worked from dawn to dusk. Since it is only in recent times that women have had any leisure at all, working is not the entire issue. The real issue is how work fits into the mother's life. In the past, mothers had their babies strapped to them and their toddlers playing at their feet while they toiled. They learned to comfort their babies as they worked. Of course, it wasn't difficult to comfort a baby, because the baby as well as the toddlers were already reassured by the mother's proximity. Babies physically bound to their mothers learned to sleep no matter what the mother was doing. Preschool-age children also benefited from always being near.

If we are to sustain this type of good attachment with our children, we must attempt to re-create this kind of successful symbiosis. In modern society this goal has been elusive until now. Because babies become very attached to their care-givers, their primary attachment to their mothers is diluted. Some children give up on their mothers and rely on their care-givers to fulfill their needs. The mothers understandably feel upset when the care-givers usurp their role. Prince William's nanny was fired because he ran to her instead of Princess Di for comfort.

Except in the special cases of mothers who work at home or mothers who are able to take their babies to their workplace at least for the first several months, surrogates must care for the babies of career women. Only 15 percent of children of working mothers are in day care. The rest have baby-sitters. Some mothers think that a loving, nurturing care-giver is as good for a child as having Mom home. In most cases, even the most unwilling mother is still the best person for raising the child. Children want their mothers. They feel deprived and let you know it in many ways if you turn them over to someone else.

So you are wondering how you can raise a child yourself if you work. It is difficult, but if you can mend the hurt of your frequent separations as you go along, you can do it well. Some mothers do this naturally. They seem to be able to reconnect with their child when they return. They know what to do to make up for their absence. They know what to expect of their child without asking too much. They have the instinct and knack to insist on the communication of feelings without sending signals that some of their child's feelings are unacceptable. Their children are free to be angry or hurt by their mother's attention to her work, so the children at least feel they are more important than the work. Their children understand the message that their mother's love is unconditional, and they feel safe. But to do all of this well all of the time would take an exceptional mother and child. Within the security of a relationship fostered by *holding time,* we all can do it.

There are several principles that are important to keep in mind if you are going to work and raise a child at the same time.

The child must be your top priority.

Make up to your child for the time you spend away.

When you are home, focus on your child. Put work out of your mind.

Truly self-reliant children are those whose needs have been met.

Accept your child's feelings about your absence and about your attention to your career.

Never allow yourself to imagine that your career is good for your child. It is your career, serving your needs.

The younger your child, the more he needs compensation for your absence.

Your child's care-giver should be someone you trust (ideally someone you would have liked as your mother).

Spend time with your child and his care-giver. Do not allow the care-giver's presence to be equated solely with your absence.

Your child must feel that he is your top priority. If you work to make ends meet, your child will understand and give you a lot of credit if you put him first the rest of the time. Even if you must work to eat, your child may still be angry about your absence. Often mothers feel unappreciated for their efforts to do everything. Be glad your child misses you and accept his feelings. If you have an elective carreer, then you must realize that your career is mostly for you. Do not fool yourself into thinking your job benefits your child in any really important way. There may be some benefits, of course. You may be happier working. Your child may place a positive value on work, seeing that you enjoy your career. Your child may have more material wealth. However, these factors are benefits only if the child does not lose the quality or the quantity of mothering he needs.

If you can stay home for a number of months after birth, do so. The more you are with your newborn, the more you will be able to foster a strong attachment between you, which can be more easily sustained when you return to work. If you can't stay home, then try to spend as much of your nonwork time as possible with your infant. Carrying packs that hold your child against your body are helpful for keeping you in touch if you must do chores after work, such as shopping. But this is not a substitute for giving your child your undivided attention when you can. You must try to make your child your first priority when you have a conflict. When your child is very ill, *you* must choose to take care of him, if humanly possible. The child will realize whether or not you put him first. If you do put him first in general, then on the occasion that you can't, he will be more likely to understand. If you always put work first, your child will feel unimportant and in the long run may have a poor self-image. Mothers often worry that they will lose their jobs or lessen their chances of promotion if they take care of their children first. There are many ways to be a good worker, but you will not have access to your greatest potential if your child is unhappy or not functional or causing trouble.

Kelly, a lawyer, came to me referred by a coworker because she was not performing well at work and was about to be fired. In fact, she was not functioning well at home either because she had been concentrating so hard on her career. Tim, her five-year-old, had a speech impediment and was always seeking attention by clowning. Ned, her eight-year-old, was becoming more and more distant. After a few months of *holding,* both boys responded to her in a way she had not imagined possible. Tim's speech improved and he began to ask for *holding* without clowning. Ned returned to his former affectionate and outgoing self. Kelly decided to start a private practice out of her home. To her surprise, she rose to the highest level of her career. Subsequently she had two more children and continued to do well in her career. *Holding time* helped to improve her effectiveness as a mother, and the feeling of success in that area made her more able to use her energy to fulfill her career aspirations as well. Working at home removed some of the strain of combining career and mothering, but her mere presence with Ned and Tim would not have been a complete remedy. More time with your children is not the whole solution unless it leads to true intimacy and better communication and connecting. If you can't provide more time, then you really need to be all the more effective in the time you do have together.

Try to make up to your child for the time you spend away. It is helpful to realize that no matter how good your child's care is, he is not as well off as if you were there full-time. If you can admit this to yourself, it will help you to make up for your absence. For example, you will be more patient and understanding. I recall watching a good friend chide her children for requiring so much of her energy on a day that she had worked hard at her career. I reminded her that they didn't ask her to have a career and didn't deserve to have her career-related problems taken out on them. As a career woman, I try to remind myself of the same thing. If we can remember that we are fortunate to be able to work and have children, it helps to keep things in perspective. It is not the children's fault that we are attempting to do so much at once. Accordingly, we must compensate them for their losses caused by our jobs.

Some working mothers automatically forgo their social life to spend as much as possible of their nonwork time with their children. Although this sacrifice is often necessary in order to give enough time to your child, I do not mean to suggest that all you have to do is be at home the rest of the time. Children need to be actively involved with you when you are home. The principle to follow here is, when you are at home, focus on your child. You may not cook elaborate meals or be an impeccable housekeeper if you also have to work. If you have to cook and do housework, either do it when your child is sleeping or do it in a way that involves a constructive interaction with your child. To do this, you can have your child play beside you as you cook or clean. Or when possible, have your child help. Even a small child can help prepare meals. Talk to your child during your chores. Try not to be caught up in doing a chore efficiently. It is more important to have a positive interaction with your child at the same time.

The moment when you come home is an important one for reconnecting with your child. Try to drop everything else. Try to forget work. Pay attention to your child. He will know that you are glad to see him and that he is very important to you. If he is your prime focus when you are home, he will think he is number one to you. His experience of your presence will be that whenever you are around, you are his. He will assume that he would always be your focus if you were always there. This impression will give him support when you are absent. On the other hand, if you come home spent or are absorbed in your chores or become annoyed with a demanding child after a long day, your child will feel that he is unimportant to you. Then two reactions are possible. He may act up, demanding more attention, most likely in a negative or even obnoxious way. You will be further frazzled. You may even dread coming home. Your relationship will enter a downward spiral. Another possible reaction from the child is withdrawal. This withdrawal can be partial or it can be quite complete. Very often mothers mistake withdrawal for developing self-reliance.

A truly self-reliant child is one whose needs have been met. You cannot really teach a child to be self-reliant. You can help him to learn how to do things himself, or sadly enough, you can leave him no choice by not helping him. But genuine, secure self-reliance happens naturally in children who have been buoyed up by adequate care, attention, and love.

Self-reliance sometimes develops well in a child whose needs are partially met. But the self-reliance can go too far and even become a somewhat spiteful rejection of the mother's help or perhaps of the mother herself. Jan and Andy are an example. Jan was widowed when Andy was a baby. She had to work full-time. By age five, Andy had developed a great deal of self-reliance. He was competent in many activities of self-care. However, he was always trying to push his limits in other ways. Jan became a nervous wreck watching Andy do stunts that seemed beyond his abilities. She was always worriedly cautioning him against injury. As a result there was always tension between them. The tension in Andy came out at night in the form of nightmares and teeth grinding and by day in defiance, stubborn-

ness, and overeating. During *holding* Jan learned that Andy felt
very exposed in the world. He felt that he had to be self-reliant
because Jan was either not with him or, when with him, not able
to judge what his abilities were. He felt totally responsible for
himself. *Holding* helped Andy to feel that his mother was taking
more care of him. He no longer felt solely responsible for himself. His need to push his own limits through daredevil stunts
diminished. Jan relaxed altogether. Andy felt free to ask for
more help from Jan. She began to do more for him even when
she knew he could do things himself.

When you are with your child, try to do the things for him
that he asks you to do. For example, tie his shoes when he asks
you to. Or accompany him to the basement when he seems
afraid to go alone. Try not to say, "You can do it yourself," or,
"You do it when I'm not here." Children who are in touch with
their feelings can guide you to do what they need. The fact that
they are asking you to do something indicates that they are
needy. The request may seem absurd to you. You may fear you
are disabling your child by babying him. Don't worry. Once the
child knows you are willing to do even things you ordinarily
would do only for a younger child, he won't feel he has to act
younger in order to obtain what he needs. The security of being
able to have any need met allows him to go forward to greater
independence because the secure interdependence he has with
you gives him the strength to let go when it counts. You won't
go wrong doing extra for your child. You may go wrong if you
don't do enough.

Many mothers worry when their children become "manipulative." I have a different view of manipulation. First of all, it is
directed toward an objective. What is the goal in the case of
children? Their goal is almost always to satisfy an unmet need.
If manipulation is done in a negative way, it usually means that
the child feels he has been unsuccessful in having his needs
filled. It should be a warning signal to you that he requires more.
In the second place, manipulation can be a positive coping

mechanism that leads to success in the outside world. Do you really want your child not to know how to manipulate to get things accomplished?

When you see your child being manipulative, ask yourself what need is unfulfilled. Meet the need before you criticize your child's expression of it. Then, to teach your child how to manipulate positively, tell him how he should ask you to meet his need and also tell him how not to. Tell him how it makes you feel when he manipulates in a negative way. Reward him for thoughtful, effective manipulation. For example, when your six-year-old child tries to extract a dollar from your husband after you have said no, tell him that you are angry that he tried to go around you. Tell him all of your reactions: anger, hurt, frustration, or disappointment. Then give him a suggestion as to how you would have wanted him to handle the situation. Ask him how he thinks he might have handled the situation better. You may discover that your child had a reason for requesting the dollar that was valid to him. Talking about it might make you agree, or it might make him feel that he didn't need the dollar after all. In any case, you will understand each other better. You will be working on a conflict resolution that does not require negative manipulation. He will see you as a reasonable, approachable person.

Three-year-old Vicky became very manipulative over tooth-brushing. She tried running away, fighting, covering her mouth, and even using somewhat precocious verbal techniques: "Now, Mom, before you brush my teeth, I have to tell you something . . ." (and something more and something more). Vicky was probably doing this to put off having to separate from her parents to go to bed; they worked, and she wanted to prolong her time with them. Discussing this problem in *holding time* was useful, especially when Vicky's mother really expressed the full force of her upset and frustration over this behavior and specified what bothered her. Later they decided together that Vicky's mom would tell an original bedtime story each night and Vicky would choose the subject. With Vicky feeling more involved in the decision, the technique chosen worked better than other ideas her parents had tried. She had a sense of a cooperative effort rather than of something forced on her. Most of the annoying manipulative behavior stopped. Vicky's mother found it easier to be firm without becoming angry whenever Vicky tried any delaying after that.

The mother viewed Vicky's manipulation as negative and responded with anger. *Holding* dealt with the mother's anger and led her to understand that the manipulative behavior was a result of Vicky's unmet need for more time with her. Without *holding* a solution might not have been reached because the mother would have remained angry at being manipulated. She would not have seen the behavior as a positive, goal-oriented maneuver on Vicky's part. They might have remained in a struggle, or Vicky might have given up trying to connect more. The next time you feel manipulated, look for your child's unmet need and try to find a way to meet it that does not anger you.

One of the most important principles of all is to accept your child's feelings about your absence and about your attention to or interest in your job. Often mothers misunderstand their children's rejection of and hostility toward their work. It really has nothing to do with the work itself. Rather they are directing hostility toward the work because it feels safer than aiming it directly toward you. They reason that they could have more of you if it weren't for your career or job. This wish might come true if you didn't work. If they blame your work, they don't have to face their anger at you.

If you discuss the issue of work while holding, you will find out what your child is thinking and feeling. You can tell him why you work. If you must work for financial reasons, say so. But be sure it is really true. If you tell your child that you work in order to live in a better house or have a fancier lifestyle, you will be teaching a value you may not want to convey. You may not want your child to think a large house is more important than family togetherness. Before you explain yourself, think about why you work and think about how you want to say it.

In any case, no matter how good your reason for working, your child will still wish he could be with you more. Force yourself to accept this wish. It is reasonable. Do not try to talk the child out of these feelings. It is good that your child wants you. Be glad. If you try to talk your child out of wanting you, it will be at the expense of his attachment to you. Tell him you understand. Tell him you will try to make up for the time away. Tell him you miss him too. Allow him to miss you. Otherwise he will force himself to repress his feelings of loss and longing. Eventually he will not allow himself to want or need you, or else he will feel frustrated and angry all of the time and act it out in undesirable ways. Either way, withdrawal or negative behavior leads the two of you into a negative interaction. Your joy in coming home will lessen. Many mothers take refuge in their work when their child expresses his distress in these ways. You do not need to take refuge in your work. You can do your work and then come home to a most rewarding experience if you will just use *holding time* to establish and maintain a mutual closeness with your child.

It is also very important that you admit to yourself that your career is for you. Of course it is good for a child to have food and shelter. But very paltry shelter and minimal food would be preferable to a child if he could have his mother home. Your standards are not his. He will feel very misunderstood if you try to convince him and yourself that your career is for him. The system a child would choose is for Daddy to work and Mommy to stay home. This is not a sexist view on the child's part. It is his need for mothering that makes him want you home.

When mothers feel guilty about being away from a child, they feel burdened by the child's need for them to be home. Don't allow yourself to be caught in a guilt trap. Instead, deal with the feelings head-on. In *holding time,* discuss your feelings and your child's feelings as well. You will find that your biggest task is to accept your child's anger. If you accept his anger, he can live with your absence. The scariest feeling for him is that you will reject him because he is angry about your absence. If he can rage at you during this intimate contact, tell you his feelings, reject you a bit by pushing you away and by telling you he prefers Daddy or saying other upsetting things, then he will feel safe knowing that you love him no matter what he feels or says to you.

The younger the child, the more difficult it is for him to deal with your absence. Therefore, be prepared to compensate more while your child is young. Be sure to make time for individual attention as often as possible. *Holding time* will give you a daily opportunity to connect on a deep and rewarding level. The resolution phase will allow you a time for a very happy exchange of love and affection.

In addition, your child needs to play with you, to be read to by you, and just to relax with you. It is not likely that a working mother can find a lot of time for this kind of togetherness during the workweek. Weekends are usually the time to schedule a special block of play. Most mothers find that meaningful time together only occurs regularly if it is carefully scheduled. Otherwise, your other responsibilities intrude and divide your attention. Be sure to allow special individual time with your children. Children learn best and derive most of their motivation for mastery from their interaction with their mothers and fathers. Siblings, peers, or care-givers cannot provide what parents can provide. Nor can playing alone compare with playing with you. However, if time does not permit both *holding time* and play, then make sure to do *holding.*

Most people can accept the idea that young children need compensation for their mothers' absence. It is much harder to recognize that older children also need it. Older children become very busy with peers and special activities. Mothers often think that the children are too busy to note their absence. Do not allow this misconception to influence your behavior. You will discover what your child needs, and you will want to fill the need. *Holding time* can be a safety net and guide. Not only do you discover your child's feelings, but the process helps elicit your positive feelings toward your child, which may have been colored by an incomplete attachment. This is especially helpful if your child is in a difficult period.

John is an example of a child with a disrupted attachment. His mother turned him over to a nanny as soon as he came home from the hospital at two weeks. Nanny took marvelous care of him and his little brother. But when John was six, the mother began to feel very threatened by his attachment to his nanny. One day he came home from school to find Nanny gone forever. His parents had fired her. John was heartbroken. Nanny had been like a grandmother to him. John never really recovered. Now that his parents are old, he is having difficulty taking good care of their needs. He is not capable of closeness either with his parents or with his wife and children. *Holding time* might have changed the history of this family if the mother had used it when she felt threatened by John's attachment to Nanny. She would have realized that Nanny was like a grandmother in John's eyes rather than like a mother. John would have more clearly demonstrated his attachment to his mother if he had reached a mutually gratifying interaction with her. Nanny would not have been suddenly dismissed. He would not have had to shut off his feelings. When he was so hurt by the loss of Nanny, he stopped trusting adults. John trusts no one in his life now. He can talk about it very analytically. But knowing all this history doesn't help him be close to his family now. He is stuck.

Your baby is primed to be attached to you. You cannot be there while you work. Therefore, you must provide as responsive and loving a substitute as possible. Then you must establish and maintain as strong a bond with your baby as you can so that you do not see a good care-giver as a threat.

A case in point is Juliet. She had two children a year apart.

Because she worked full-time as a consultant, she hired a full-time housekeeper, who adored both of the girls and took care of them as well as a devoted grandmother would. Juliet became intensely jealous of her daughters' relationship with the house-keeper, even though the babies were still responsive to her despite her spending only an hour a day with them. Sadly, Juliet fired the housekeeper and placed the girls in day care, where there was no threat of deep attachment.

Mothers, you can't have it both ways. Either you must stay home to be the sole caretaker, or you must provide an adequate substitute and then do your best to be your child's main source of attachment. If there is no alternative to day care, don't become bogged down in guilt. Just realize that you have to do that much more compensating. Luckily, both the closeness and the channel of communication provided by *holding time* will go very far toward compensating for even the most difficult circumstances. No matter how much you cede your child's care to someone else, your child will prefer you. You can detach, but almost nothing anyone else can do will lead to your child's transfer of attachment. If you maintain a strong tie with your child, he will not feel maternally deprived.

Sometimes mothers feel that they must deliver their child over to the care-giver in order to assure that the care-giver will be motivated to attend to the child. You may feel guilty about asking the care-giver to take over while you are away but to step back when you are there. Don't feel guilty. The care-giver will have a better relationship with your child if the child is well attached to you. When a child has a solid primary attachment, he relates much better to another person, whether the other is his father, grandmother, or baby-sitter. Children with faulty mother-child bonding have difficulty with all relationships.

Through *holding time,* Amy's ability to discuss her feelings was extended to her relationships with other people. One day when Nanny was driving her to a playground, Amy said, "Nanny, please stop the car. I want to talk to you." Nanny said,

"You can talk while I drive. I'll listen." Amy said, "No, I want to look in your eyes." She had learned how good it feels to make good eye contact while discussing important feelings. So Nanny pulled over to the side of the road. For about half an hour, Amy and Nanny discussed Amy's distress over her mother's leaving for work three and a half days a week. Amy said to Nanny that she was mad when Nanny arrived and Mommy left. Nanny asked, "Are you happy when Mommy comes home and I leave?" Amy said yes. Nanny said, "I will always listen to your angry feelings, but you must also tell your mommy these feelings during *holding time.*" Because of Nanny's understanding that anger is to be expressed and discussed, she was able first to tolerate and second to handle Amy's feelings without getting angry herself at Amy's implied rejection of her. Amy was so gratified by Nanny's response that she told her, "Nanny, I love you. Will you come on vacation with us?" Nanny reports that she can tell the difference in Amy when she has been held and when she has not. You can see that Amy now has a way of dealing with her feelings that goes beyond *holding time.* She has learned how to confront her feelings freely. As a result, Nanny is able to respond in a helpful way. Unfortunately, mothers cannot expect all baby-sitters to be like this one.

There is no more common topic among working mothers than the problem of child care, which is often high-priced yet unsatisfactory. Nevertheless, you can overcome many of the problems by careful screening of potential baby-sitters and then by helping the person you hire to fit into your family in the most satisfactory way. When you choose a care-giver, try to hire someone whom you feel like treating as a member of the family. First of all, this guideline will help you choose a pleasant and loving person. Second, it is important for your child to feel that the person who is so important to his daily well-being is someone you admire, respect, and care for. I do not mean that the person should match you in background, education, or even culture. I mean that the person should be someone you trust. If you can't stand to be around a person, do not choose her for your child's care-giver. Try to find out her history before you hire her. Ask her about her own upbringing. First find out about the quality and nature of her own mother's relationship with her. Try to find out about her feelings for her father, particularly if you have a boy. Does she have siblings? If she has a brother whom she hated or felt jealous toward, be careful if you have a boy. Find out what her attitudes are about women and herself. She will convey these attitudes to your child. Discover her beliefs about children's discipline, toilet training, eating, and sleeping. Assume that you may not be able to teach her new attitudes. Does she have a capacity for warmth and love for children? How does she feel about her job caring for children? Is it her job because she can't do anything else, or does she prefer this job to others? Be courageous in asking as many of the above questions as you can force yourself to ask. You are not just being nosy. The woman you hire will be entrusted with your most precious possession, and she will influence your child by her attitudes, her prejudices, and the way she was nurtured. Try to make sure in advance that she has the qualities you want brought into contact with your family.

Chester was a seven-year-old who couldn't behave in school. His parents were somewhat older people and delighted to have a little boy when they did. Both were busy with careers. However, they did spend a good deal of time with Chester on weekends. Chester told me that his parents "kicked [him] around like an old shoe." From what I knew of his parents, the source of his problems wasn't apparent. It became evident when I met the baby-sitter, a belligerent, unhappy-looking woman with no patience for a young child.

Another important aspect of your choice of care-giver is continuity. Because you are fostering an important attachment between your child and the care-giver, you must make sure the tie between them lasts as long as possible. Too many broken attachments lead to an unwillingness to form new ones. A cycle of mistrust is started that carries well beyond childhood.

Some care-givers are not good no matter what you do to support them. Some, however, are very good if you fill some of their needs. Most mothers who work do not realize that the care-giver needs care, because they rarely catch a glimpse of what goes on when they are away. Listening to a report of the day and complimenting the care-giver may be one shortcut to a well-functioning home.

Here is a warning. If you come home and your care-giver remains in charge, either by your child's designation, hers, or yours, something is wrong. Your child will immediately confer upon you the job of care-giver if there is no problem between you. If he doesn't, *holding time* will get you back together. If your care-giver remains in charge after you come home, it may be that she senses that you do not want to take over. Often a career woman returning from work is exasperated from her long day. You may be giving your substitute a message that you are not to be bothered. Or if you aren't giving that message, she may be aware of the lack of connection between you and your child and may just be trying to fill the gap. The more intuitive she is, the more apt she will be to try to fill in. If you establish good communication with her, you may be able to discuss some of these issues.

An unusually happy example of a career woman's good relationship with her substitute is Betty's relationship with Greta. In fact Greta was not Betty's first choice. Because Betty was not an experienced interviewer, she did not elicit the information that would have indicated what a great care-giver Greta could be. By chance the first choice did not work out, and luckily Greta was still available. Betty was practicing *holding* regularly and she made sure Greta saw and understood it. Now, because she realizes how important mother-child communication is, Greta writes a detailed report of her and her little charge's activities and conversations of the day. She gently suggests more mother-child *holding* sessions when they seem needed. She has a satisfying job because she is working with a happy, well-behaved child who can return her love. She feels she is really helping the mother maintain her connection with the child. Of course, Betty is very appreciative and shows it, and Greta is fulfilled in her work.

It is also desirable for you to spend some time with your child and his care-giver together. First of all, you have to spend time in order to have a mutual interchange with her. Second, and very important, her presence should not always be equated with your absence. Betty finally came to that conclusion and has arranged to spend time at home when Greta is there. Actually it was her child who alerted her to the equation: Greta's presence is equal to Mommy's absence. Betty now spends half the morning at home while Greta is there. Not many mothers who work can stay home mornings, so they may have to ask the care-giver to stay later when they return from work. It is good to include the care-giver in a child's life at other times, such as a birthday party or a special event. If the care-giver is a part of family life, it adds to a child's sense of security.

The principles discussed in this chapter can act as guidelines for working and raising children simultaneously. The main goal is to maintain a strong attachment with your children in spite of constant separations. If you can keep mending the hurt of separations as you go along, you will be able to combine work and mothering successfully. *Holding time* will establish more open communication of feelings, which allows your child to perceive that he is more important than your work and that he is free to be angry or hurt about your absence without negative repercussions. You child will feel that he is safe because of what he perceives to be your unconditional love. If you can achieve this, you will develop a mutually gratifying and guilt-free relationship while you continue working.

12.

THE DIVORCING MOTHER
AND THE
DISINTEGRATING CHILD
How You Can Minimize the
Damage of Divorce and What
the Father Can Do to Help

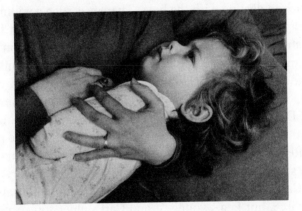

Divorce poses a threat to a child's security, and a child whose security is in question invariably reacts in ways that indicate how upset he is. The problem for the mother is that the child's reaction usually includes negative behavior that she is least able to handle at a moment when she herself is devastated by the divorce. No matter what the circumstances of the divorce, it is a disruptive, destructive process for all members of the family. Saying that divorce is destructive is not saying that no parents should divorce or that nothing good can come of it. I can think of families who have worked through the destruction in a positive way with eventual good results. However, they used *holding time* to protect against the weakening of the parent-child bond that usually occurs during this time of conflict.

Don and Karen came for help in the midst of their first separation struggles. Karen felt like running away from both Don and their two sons. She had always felt that Don was a better father than she was a mother. The children had already begun to show signs of distress. The four-year-old was acting more and more babyish and the seven-year-old was beginning to withdraw. Karen began *holding* with their sons. They all survived the divorce functioning well. Both Karen and Don remarried. All four partners came for sessions together to reach a united approach to dealing with the boys. There was such a willingness to work together that they were even able to have joint family celebrations of important events. This kind of cooperation is the best situation possible for children of divorce. Don, his new wife, and Karen's new husband all worked together, in effect, to support Karen's mothering, and at the same time they supported Don's fathering and the new spouses' stepparenting.

Another family made use of *holding time* to pick up the pieces long after divorce. Peg and Carl had married several years after their respective divorces. Peg had three girls from her first marriage, Carl two boys. All five children had suffered because of the divorce, but Peg's youngest and Carl's older son seemed to need the most repair. Peg used *holding* with both of these children. This is an unusual example, because it was the older boy's stepmother who did the *holding* with him. Let me add that it was this child's request that his stepmother hold him after he saw the process and the results with his youngest stepsister. This is an important point because it might not work in another situation, where the child would feel that the stepmother had "kidnapped" him from his mother. Certainly in the case of Karen and Don, it could have caused terrible trouble for Karen or the children to feel that the stepmother was trying to take her place.

As we have noted previously, the most important thing a

father can do for a child is to love the child's mother. A step-father can play an extremely important surrogate role in a step-child's life in the absence of the biological father. By loving, supporting, and attending to the mother, the stepfather provides for the child what the absent father cannot. The father does not need to feel eclipsed by the stepfather. If he could be completely objective, he would appreciate the role of his ex-wife's new husband. Nevertheless, a divorced father still has an important role to play with his ex-wife as well as with his children. A father can be divorced and still try to be supportive of his ex-wife's mothering. He can do this first by making sure he does not act as though he wants to take the children away from her, either physically or psychologically. Second, even though divorced, a couple can and should agree upon a consistent code of behavior that they expect of their children. Finally, the father can still provide an ear for the mother's complaints about having to raise the children under difficult conditions.

You may have noticed that I haven't mentioned financial support. Many fathers do not pay any child support after five years. Of course it would be preferable if they did, but given this reality, it seems even more practical to work on the other aspects of family management during and after the divorce. Perhaps if the other aspects were worked out amicably, more fathers would continue to give financial support longer.

In order to achieve a good father-mother working relationship in divorce, pride has to take a backseat. One is not giving in or losing when the best interests of parents and children are served in the long run. It is very important for partners to tell each other what has made them angry, what has led to disappoint-ment, what was painful. They should also tell each other what has been good about their relationship. If the parties cannot do this face-to-face, they should at least do it in writing. Thereafter, they should keep this somewhat balanced picture in mind. The reasons for putting a great deal of effort into this exercise are twofold. First, it will help the mother and father deal with their feelings and with each other. Second, it will help each one allow the children to love the other.

One very quick way to alienate a child from you is to denigrate the other parent. If the parent has faults, the child will see them soon enough. If you criticize your ex-spouse to the child, he will be so busy defending the parent under attack that he may blind himself to even the most obvious inadequacies. Another consequence is a negative impact on that parent's value as a role model. If you, the mother, denigrate the father to his son, the boy will feel inferior insofar as he identifies with his father as a male, which he must do in order to achieve normal male development. Later your son may even seek a wife who denigrates him to duplicate the model of woman and wife he learned from you. If you belittle the father to his daughter, you may be laying the groundwork for her to choose a man who matches *your* image of her father. Then she will belittle him in her marriage. It is dismaying to see to what extent people repeat the negative patterns of their early family life.

If a father criticizes a mother to a child, he is instructing that child to have low regard for the mother and not to obey her. This only leads to lack of control for the child, which becomes even more dangerous as the teen years approach, especially with the father absent from the home. Furthermore, if the father maligns the mother to a girl, he impairs her self-image insofar as she identifies with the mother, which she must do in order to achieve normal female development. If the father maligns a boy's mother, the boy will feel guilty for loving her and devalue his own feelings. After all, he loves his mother but his father despises the mother, so how can he trust his feelings? Then, too, he may extend his father's attitude to all women. Such a child will be in trouble as a husband and father later in life.

If two parents can emerge from a divorce with even a little show of respect for each other, they will feel better about themselves too. After all, they chose each other. It is devastating to have to invalidate a whole marriage. Anyone who married, had children, and spent some years with another person must have had some positive feelings for the other's attributes.

One of the largest stumbling blocks to a positive resolution of divorce is pride. If you are divorcing, try to put pride at the bottom of your list of priorities. Pride is totally destructive in conflict resolution. Try to ask yourself on every issue what is most important, pride or the long-term well-being of you and your children.

Keeping all this theory in mind, let's turn to a very important issue: how will you know what is best for your child? You will develop a better sense of what is good for your child when you have a mutually gratifying relationship with him that makes open communication a daily possibility.

Take Teddy, for example. His parents separated when he was three years old. His father went through a very rough period lasting about two years. During this period he was unable to pay attention to Teddy when they were together. When Teddy was four, he told his mother during *holding* that he wanted someone with him when he was with Daddy. He asked that either of his grandparents or his mother be there during his play with his father. Because Teddy was an aware child who was in touch with his feelings, his mother took the request seriously. She explained the request to the father, who was able to listen to it because he knew that his ex-wife was not trying to upset him but rather to take care of their son. He also knew from the son's wonderful ability to communicate his feelings that he didn't say something lightly or in a complaining way. He knew that Teddy was always direct. As it turned out, they did have a better time together when other family members were present. A few years later when the father remarried, Teddy said that he had a better time with his father when the new wife was there too. He said that she improved his father's personality and his behavior toward him.

Had this couple not reached a good working divorce relationship, they could not have given their child the understanding and support he was asking for. The father would not have discovered the problem without the mother, or if he had, he might have discounted the child's feelings as having been determined by the mother's influence.

If you aim for a good working relationship, you might achieve it. If you don't expect it or believe it possible, you will never reach your goal. You should try, just to satisfy yourself that you have done everything possible to create the best environment for yourself and your children. And if you try, you will be providing your children with a good example. They may copy you, and in any case they will respect and appreciate your efforts, whether you succeed or not. Also, you will know how best to help your child with his feelings about the divorce, his dad, himself, yourself, or anything else that comes along, if you have open communication.

You may not be able to work out a good system with the father. You may in fact remain at war with him. Nevertheless, *holding time* can help you strengthen and maintain a strong bond with your child in spite of the destructive process of divorce. It gives your child a safe channel into which to direct his anger, his hurt, his disappointment, his fears about the divorce.

Ginger had been estranged from her father since the time of the parental separation. The father had no idea why this child did not want to see him, because the other three came often. In fact, one incident at the time of the separation had so hurt and frightened Ginger that she dared not go near him. He had spanked her for what he thought was unacceptable behavior—hoarding food—but she had been afraid that they would not have money for food after he left. If he or the mother had been in good communication with her and with each other, they could have reassured her instead of punishing her. She would have been relieved, she would have felt understood, and she would not have been alienated. *Holding time* would not have allowed this situation to develop, as the fears would have been exposed and allayed before the negative behavior had occurred.

Children often feel that they are somewhat responsible for a divorce. Such feelings come out during *holding.* Children usually are reluctant to take sides. As a consequence, they often clam up. *Holding time* will ensure that they have a chance to deal with all of their feelings in a safe way. Often children are afraid that you will leave them too. If you can separate from Dad, can you separate from them too? *Holding* conveys a reassuring message that no matter what feelings they have, you will love them. This message is hard for a child to believe when he sees that it really didn't work out that way with you and his father. Therefore, children of divorce need this reassurance all the more. When they see that they really can bring all of their feelings to you without being rejected, they will begin to relax.

Sometimes mothers are afraid of putting ideas into their children's heads, especially in the case of a young child. Be assured that any child old enough to talk is old enough to profit from discussing feelings, and no child is too old for it. You can rarely make a mistake by trying to guess how your child feels. He will be relieved that you are trying. He will know that you think his feelings are important. He will consciously recognize that feelings are there inside of him. He will work to search them out. Children do not adopt a feeling that you have suggested unless it rings true. Sometimes a child does not realize what his feelings are until you help him think about them. He will pass over a wrong guess and wait for you to hit the mark. The important principle is to keep trying. Sometimes mothers are afraid to start *holding time* because the children might tell the fathers, who in turn might object to it. This happened in one family that I know, with surprising results.

Jill and Tim separated with much bitterness after a long, unhappy marriage. At the time of Jill and their eight-year-old son Eddie's move to a different house, Eddie completely lost control of his feelings and began to assault children at school. When he was expelled, Jill sought *holding* therapy. After one session, which lasted about five hours, Jill felt a connection with Eddie that she hadn't experienced since his infancy. The father heard about this session and decided to go to court to prevent further therapy. However, Jill and Eddie felt so much better that she became constructively assertive with her husband. He began to back down. Then when he saw the dramatic improvement in Eddie, he lost his resolve to block the help. Jill and Eddie continued both the therapy and *holding time* at home. In this case, the good results improved the mother-child situation so much that the father got no leverage from it.

What so often happens in divorce is that the children disintegrate emotionally because their hurt, fear, and anger are all-consuming, sapping all the energy that would have gone into good functioning. They become hostile, belligerent, and seemingly unreachable. The mother herself is extremely stressed by the pressures of divorce: the grief of loss, if only the loss of a dream, the humiliation of failure, the fear of the future alone, the anger at the ex-husband for his sins of omission and commission, the disappointment. She is no doubt trying to earn a living and, at the same time, run a household alone; she may be trying to have a social life or forming a new relationship with a man. Rarely can she also fight the battle required to reach a recalcitrant child. Nor does she have any idea how to do it if she could find the energy and motivation.

It seems that the older the child is, the more severe the problems can be. Why is this so? Younger children have a primary need for a mother. If the mother can create even a modicum of stability, she can maintain enough connection with the children to keep them from regressing. Of course, a mother of young children can fall apart so that she can't even do this, and the more the father was involved in their care, the more disruptive is his departure. However, older children are much more sensitive to the departure of the father even if he wasn't greatly involved in their care. If the children do visit the father regularly, such as every other weekend, they are in another type of bind. They are angry with the father for his perceived abandonment of them. They are with him only enough to recapture their pain but not really enough to offset the loss. And they suffer from not being with the mother during that time. They feel hurt that she sent them away, even though they want to be with the father. It's important to understand these conflicting sentiments. Unless you understand the mixed feelings your child will have, you will not be able to help him sort them out and reach a resolution. Then, too, unless you understand the conflicts, you will be angry with your child unnecessarily. For example, children usually come home from a weekend with Dad feeling very irritable and usually hostile toward the mother. The mother assumes that the child is misbehaving because of the way the father handled him over the weekend or, worse, that the father has been bad-mouthing her to the child. It isn't necessarily so. Even if the father took good care of the child and spent meaningful time with him, the child could come home in a state of distress. The good time could have revived his longing to have his father at home. And the absence of the mother could have registered as maternal deprivation for him.

Danny's father took him to his home every other weekend and one night a week. Although his dad was very attentive, Danny invariably returned home very keyed up and usually was unable to fall asleep that night. His mother always got mad at the father, assuming that he had stirred up the boy. In reality this eight-year-old was strained to his limit by the long daily separations caused by the mother's work and other life activities. He really couldn't afford a weekend away from his mother. He needed that time to make up for the rest of the week's deficits. Since the age of three, he had been spending the majority of his weekends with his father. When the schedule was changed to every other weekend, Danny seemed to feel a little better. The mother had difficulty accepting Danny's feelings about his time away because she needed the break so much herself. *Holding* could have helped her to deal with her feelings as well as with Danny's.

I have said earlier that *holding time* is just as beneficial to mothers as it is to children. Divorce is a situation in which it is crucial to the mother's well-being. You need love, affection, and mutual closeness. Without a spouse, you will be operating at a deficit. Holding a child can help to compensate. In this way, divorcing mothers are more fortunate than divorcing fathers, because they have a natural source of love and fulfillment in the children. The father loses this source when he moves out.

It is important to realize that your child can be a source of closeness and fulfillment for you. Some mothers worry that they are using their children. My work with mothers and children has convinced me that anytime the mother is not receiving satisfying feedback and some payoff from the mother-child relationship, the connection is not complete. A strong mother-child bond affords the mother as much gratification as it does the child. So if you aren't feeling that your relationship with your child is feeding you and buoying you up, *holding time* can help.

You may wonder how to find time for this system in the middle of a chaotic life. When can you do it with everything else in your life taking precedence? I admit it is difficult. Cheryl, a mother of six children, taught me a lesson I will never forget. Her success underscores the power of a little *holding.* She came to me complaining of depression. She and her husband were separated. He did not support the family at all. She had a full-time job and couldn't deal with the stress of her disintegrating home life. When I told her to hold, she was dumbfounded by the prospect of finding time and motivation to approach five big sons and one daughter. Not really having a full grasp of what kind of stress she must have been under, I just insisted that she find the time. Two weeks later Cheryl returned for a follow-up appointment. She was radiant. She reported that she had taken my advice as best she could, and everything had turned out just the way I had said it would. Now it was my turn to be dumbfounded. She said that she had held each child for ten minutes each day. They liked it and demanded that she give each of them the full ten minutes, not eight or nine. Now they were all cooperating with each other and with her to run the house. Cheryl's depression gradually lifted as she connected more and more with her kids.

One difficulty is that you, the mother, need the father's support. If he is gone, even if he backs you in theory, you don't have his concrete support. Some mothers have found their own parents helpful as a father substitute in *holding time.* If your parents live nearby, try to enlist their aid. Other mothers use close friends for backing. Some mothers have no difficulty using *holding* on their own because the positive outcome so clearly offsets the added difficulty of doing it unsupported. And you must remember that on the other side of the enhanced communication is a closeness so rewarding and a relationship with your child so gratifying that it is worth the struggle. You can't afford more stress when you are divorcing. Luckily, you will find that just the act of *holding* itself reduces your stress level. It is just as good for a mother as for a child. And, of course, the relief it gives your child will prevent the misbehavior he otherwise probably would exhibit.

How then do you use this method with children of divorce? First, you will have to do it alone for the most part. Second, you will have to be extra strong, because children are likely to say that they prefer Daddy when their mothers hold them. This kind of statement is painful enough when you are safely married to Daddy. If you are divorcing, it can be devastating. But being forewarned should help. You might reply that you know your child is angry at you for the divorce. If he sees that the worst rejection (which saying he prefers Daddy is meant to be) does not put you off, then he will feel safer. Also, you must tell him how you feel when he says that. You might say, "I feel very hurt, angry, and rejected when you say you prefer Daddy." If you can show him by crying or by the hurt inflection in your voice, he will probably respond in a comforting way. We find that children respond immediately when their mothers show them the deepest hurt or despair. As long as the mother appears strong, they seem to hold out. When the mother caves in, they come to her rescue.

Mothers are always amazed at how the expression of their true feelings invariably elicits a heartfelt response from their child. Often this kind of experience is new to mothers. Because their connection was not as good as it could have been, they never had realized that it would be possible for their child to respond to *them*. They often didn't know to what extent a mother-child relationship could be mutual. They had thought it was their job to respond to the child's needs but not that the child should respond to theirs. So many mothers report feeling that all they ever did was give, give, give. This is not the way it should be! If you feel this way, you need to start *holding* immediately and do it until you feel that your relationship is mutual.

Interdependence is the most important goal. Undoubtedly, failure to achieve interdependence in your marriage was a major determinant of your divorce. Maybe you thought that independence was the most important goal. You have probably pushed your child toward it. You may even be afraid that you can't achieve independence yourself now that you are divorced. Please forget independence. Most everyone can achieve it. The difficult achievement is mutual interdependence. In any case, you can't push someone to independence. If they have a good enough base, the ability to be independent will come naturally. If you give your child an intimate, gratifying relationship with you, you will be paving the way for harmonious relations with everyone he chooses to work or live with in the future. In this way, you will be insuring against the trauma of divorce. Your well-being depends on your child's well-being and vice versa. There is a saying that a mother is only as happy as her unhappiest child. This saying may not be absolute, but in my clinical practice it is often true.

In any case, if you ensure your child's well-being through *holding time,* your new single life will be easier. You will be spared the difficulties of living with a disturbed, disruptive, or even destructive child. You will receive the nurturing that stems from a mutually gratifying relationship. You will have less interference with your work and social life.

The pain of loss is great no matter what the circumstances. I have even seen children suffer from the loss of an abusive parent. Children usually love a parent whether or not the parent deserves it. It is natural. You must keep in mind that your child is feeling pain. Many things that may not seem to you to have any bearing on the loss will revive the pain for the child. You need to have patience with these recurrent feelings. *Holding* helps mothers have patience. In fact, an excellent occasion for *holding time* is when *you* are feeling impatient. Children usually reveal the cause of their pain when you hold them. It is amazing how much more children will and can communicate when given this channel than when they are merely conversing.

The role of the divorcing father can be crucial. If you are a father who is watching a child disintegrate because of the mother's actions and reactions to divorce or remarriage, you may wonder if you can help with *holding time.* If you are on cordial terms with your ex-wife, you could ask her to read this book. If not, perhaps you could ask a mutual friend or relative to give it to her. And you can make extra efforts to support her mothering.

Charles is a good example of a father who is helping his daughter by giving all the backing possible to her mother. He does this by taking the child whenever the mother needs help, giving as much financial support as he can to make his ex-wife's life easier, being sympathetic about her problems with the troubled child, keeping in close contact with the child's school, and maintaining a very strong tie with his child by using *holding* and by spending meaningful time with her. When he is with his daughter, he devotes his full attention to her. He plans activities that she can enjoy with him. He encourages her mastery of skills and sports. He sets limits on her behavior so that she does not feel out of control, and he uses *holding* to give her an outlet for her feelings. He gives her a great deal of physical affection. Even so, he cannot entirely compensate for the disturbed mother-child relationship. But he is offering as much stability and security and intimacy as he can under difficult conditions. His child has a model of good parenting that may help her when she is a parent. She may be able to find a husband like her father who can love her and offer her stability. Despite the difficulties, Charles takes a great joy in his little daughter. As a result, the child relates well to the mother. In addition, all this good fathering makes the mother feel better. Mothers nurture better when people, especially fathers and grandparents, show interest in their child. This father is careful and tactful so that the mother does not feel threatened; otherwise she might try to limit their contact. Even if she didn't, there might be a constant struggle, which would have negative effects on the child.

This system practiced by either or both parents in divorce will diminish the effects of disrupted attachments. Despite any negative circumstances, it helps you to establish and maintain an intimate, mutually gratifying relationship with your child, which paves the way for your child to have positive relationships with everyone else in his present and future life. *Holding time* is protection against the devastating effects of divorce.

13.

THE DEPRESSED MOTHER
AND THE
DISTRESSED CHILD
How You Can Protect Your Child
from Your Mood

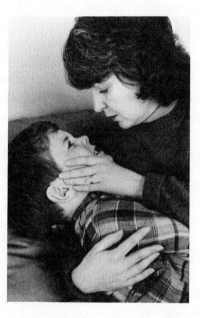

Most mothers have some feelings of depression at one time or another. Depression is usually triggered by feelings of loss. The loss can be a concrete event, such as the death of a loved one. Or it can be a perceived loss of love, such as when someone important to you withdraws from you in anger or merely in a necessary separation that is only temporary, such as a husband's short-term assignment in another city. The loss can also be a relative decrease in someone's love and attention, as, for example, when a new baby arrives. Some mothers' depression begins during their childhood and recurs when they become mothers.

When a mother feels depressed, she is less able to function. She simply does not feel like functioning. Depressed mothers usually withdraw into themselves. Some people respond to depression with sleeplessness, in which case they suffer all the additional consequences of sleep deprivation, including irritability, sensitivity, and impatience, none of which helps mothering. Some people respond to depression by sleeping a great deal. This response poses special difficulties for children because they lose their mother's availability.

Children are very responsive to their mother's emotional state. Therefore, when Mommy is depressed, they want to do something to make it better. However, it is very difficult to help a depressed person to feel better. Consequently, the child feels not only a loss and a lack of connection but also helplessness and inadequacy. He cannot justify anger toward his depressed mother. Yet his needs remain unmet. His anger then is turned on himself, and he may become depressed. He may also become depressed because he identifies with his mother. In other words, the child learns to be depressed by the mother's example.

The most extreme example I know of a child's copying a parent's way of handling life is a little boy named Billy. Billy's parents were blind. No one was alarmed when blindness was diagnosed in Billy. He was well nurtured by his parents and developed well enough to be placed in a normal nursery school, where he fit right in with the sighted children. One day some fire trucks were outside the school. Little Johnny said, "Billy, come quick to look at the fire engines." The teacher went over to Johnny to explain that Billy was blind and what blindness was. Johnny replied, "Oh, no, teacher. Billy is not blind. He just doesn't know how to use his eyes." It turned out that Johnny was correct. Billy had perfect vision. He had merely learned how to cope without the use of sight because he so completely mimicked his parents. The moral of the story is: think about how you behave, because your children will surely copy you.

Holding time can help spare a child from the usual consequences of having a depressed mother by helping him to feel connected with her. At least during this special contact the child will not be suffering the loss of his mother. On the contrary, he will experience deep connection with her during the resolution. In addition, *holding* keeps children from feeling inadequate by giving them an outlet for all of their feelings. If a mother can hold on until the resolution, the child will feel that he and his feelings are acceptable. He will not devalue himself, because his feelings won't have to be disowned, repressed, suppressed, or denied.

A child will not feel helpless, because he will have an effective way of making contact with his mother. Moreover, he will feel very good because the close contact will improve his mother's condition. It provides a safe and constructive avenue for the expression of anger. When anger is constructively channeled, it is not left to be turned against the self. The source of the anger is not really important. The mother can express her anger and sadness during *holding* with her child. At first this may sound unfair to the child, but in fact he will be greatly relieved to discover that he is not the cause of her depression.

Most important for the mother, *holding time* gives her a way of making a deep and rewarding bond with her child. One deep tie is enough to steady a person and make life worth living. When the mother is gratified by being able to connect with her child, she has a source for better self-esteem. Improved self-esteem will lead to better function, and better function will lead to even better self-esteem. She may also receive a great deal of positive feedback from other people because she has a happy, well functioning child who can love others.

Pam, a thirty-five-year-old mother of two daughters, a four-month-old and a two-year-old, came to me because her husband was exasperated with her inability to take care of their home.

She was not complaining of depression but was in fact severely depressed by anyone's standards. She reported that she had been lonely during her pregnancy but hardly aware of it at the time. Once she returned home after giving birth, nothing seemed to improve. She was exhausted. She described feeling that she was in a nightmare that would never end. The two-year-old was ruling the roost in an angry, obnoxious way. Her husband was preoccupied by a career change. The new baby was unresponsive. Pam, feeling out of control, was having difficulty getting along with everyone. *Holding time* saved Pam and her family from the effects of her depression. She said, "*Holding* has turned my entire life around. Not only has it made my baby responsive and loving, but it has saved my older daughter by letting her have an outlet for her feelings. She knows that she can share them all with me and anything goes. She trusts me and probably has truly bonded for the first time. *Holding* requires a fantastic amount of energy and perseverance. It is not for the lazy or those who do not want to take responsibility. But the fact is that it works. All family members are in touch with each other. I've learned to allow myself to have feelings in a way I had never experienced. Now it is a natural part of my life."

Imagine how you would have felt and what you would have said during the rejection phase if you had been *holding* with each of your parents. Imagine what they would have replied to you when they heard what you had said. Imagining *holding* through the three phases with them will make you aware of the issues between you and your feelings aroused by those issues. Awareness can then help you when you are dealing with these important people. Instead of reacting automatically, you will be better able to choose how you wish to act and react. You will feel much more in control of your interactions and therefore your life. The feelings of helplessness, which were part of your depression, will be changed to feelings of power, if only over yourself. Of course, when you have control over yourself, you have a great deal more influence over others.

As Jean, a depressed mother of three, said after *holding time* had improved her depression, "*Holding* takes the emphasis off myself and makes me realize I am responsible for others. Not all of us recognize our own depression. When I saw how depressed I was, I realized I had felt that way all my life. I had always thought I had a perfect relationship with my mother. But loving each other was not enough. *Holding* with my daughters enabled me to ask my mother for what I need from her now. In turn I can give her more of what she wants and needs from me. Now I realize how important I am. And now I know what to watch for in my mother-daughter relationships."

You too may find that your needs can be met better because you are able to connect with the people who are important to you. Your feelings of isolation will turn into feelings of closeness with your loved ones. Because you are more gratified, you will be less depressed. Your inability to act will change to an increasing desire and ability to function effectively. Feelings of closeness with a loved one act as fuel to power the drive for fulfillment of one's potential, whether as a parent, a worker, a friend, or even a hobbyist. Speaking of hobbies, it is important to remember the importance of play in our lives. Depressed people often feel undeserving of good times as well as of good relations. It is useful to pursue a hobby or some kind of fun on a regular basis, whether at first you feel like it or not. Once you start, you will probably enjoy it. If you do it with one of your children, you will increase your chances of closeness as well as your enjoyment of the activity.

Now let's look at depression in children. Formerly it was thought that children did not experience depression the way adults do. Today, depression in children is recognized and understood, especially as a reaction to disturbing situations and life events.

For example, childhood depression is common in the siblings

of children with serious problems requiring a great deal of the parents' attention. No matter how much the parents care about the well child, circumstances require that they take care of the child with the problem. The well child feels a loss of the attention he had been enjoying and helplessness at not being able to change the situation. Sometimes such siblings develop actual physical problems as a way of attracting attention. More commonly, they have psychosomatic complaints or school difficulties because of an underlying depression. *Holding time* goes a long way toward bringing these children out of depression. It gives them a concentrated dose of the attention they feel they are missing. It gives them a healthy outlet for their feelings and brings them into intimate contact with their parents.

Children in unhappy marriages often suffer depression because their connection with the parents is not supported by a good mother-father attachment. They usually have some loss of attachment with their mother, who is disturbed by her unhappiness. The father often has difficulty maintaining contact with a child if he is not well connected to the mother.

Depression is usual in children of divorce. It is also common in children with learning disabilities or any other kind of handicap. Depression is unavoidable for children who lose a parent or a sibling.

However, the most common cause of depression in children is a mother whose own depression puts a strain on the mother-child attachment. The child of a depressed mother suffers a partial loss of the mothering and has a depressed person for a very important role model as well. You can help prevent this situation by *holding*.

Holding time helps protect a child from learning a depressive mode of living and diminishes the negative effect of a mother's depression by helping her maintain a good mother-child attachment. It helps you shield your child from depression, at the same time lifting your spirits and giving you both a more satisfying relationship.

14.

THE SIBLING RIVALS
AND THE
EXASPERATED MOTHER
How to Create Harmony
in Your Home

Do you often wonder why your children get along so much better when you are not around? In most families there is some squabbling, some degree of aggressive behavior, some tattling, and some excessive competition among siblings. This rivalry can be one of the most difficult and unpleasant aspects of parenting.

In finding a solution to sibling rivalry, it is most important to realize that your children are competing over you because of unmet needs and that meeting the needs usually diminishes the rivalry. Those of you who value a sense of competition have no need to worry; a healthy competitive drive is not the same as sibling rivalry. In fact, some children are so conflicted over sibling rivalry that their energies are not free to be channeled into healthy competition. For example, when one child feels that the other is favored, he usually has lower self-esteem. High self-esteem is the best facilitator of the drive for accomplishment. To the extent that you can resolve the rivalry among your children, you will be freeing their energy for constructive pursuits. If your sons are playing basketball to see who makes the most points, fiercely but pleasantly vying with each other and generally having a good time, you know they are competing in a healthy way. On the other hand, if you hear angry yelling— "You cheated! Stop it!" "No, you fouled me!" "Mom, Bill's not playing fair!"—then you know these boys are not functioning optimally. It's certain you don't want to be around when they are playing basketball. Everyone feels alienated from everyone else.

The main solution lies in helping build your children's self-esteem by giving them adequate love and attention. When you have more than one child, giving each enough is a big problem. Parents love their children; most parents pay some attention to them. Often, however, the quantity and quality are not adequate. When a child's need is not met, he becomes hurt and angry. The feelings are expressed in negative behavior, often directed at a sibling. *Holding time* provides a more constructive outlet for upset feelings than negative behavior does. The child is allowed to blow up and complain. The mother has a chance to express her exasperation with the negative behavior and her hurt over the constant bickering and aggression. The mother then feels more able to sympathize with the child's feelings. It is extremely important for parents to acknowledge the child's anger toward a sibling even though, in the heat of the moment, it is not easy to do. During *holding*, however, it is easier to separate your disapproval of negative behavior from your acceptance of the child's feelings, because he is safely contained in your arms, not carrying out the aggressive action.

When Tommy, a toddler, physically attacked his baby sister, their mother had to stop the dangerous action; this response was emotional and direct, with no time taken to make allowance for the toddler's feelings. But when the mother put the baby in a safe place and then held the toddler in a tight embrace, she was free to discuss feelings like this: "Tommy, I know you are angry with Leelee. You have to wait for her to be fed or diapered or rocked to sleep. It must be very hard for you to wait. You need more attention from me." Tommy fought and cried. His mother told him how upset she feels when he hits the baby. She explained why he can't be allowed to do it but that she loves him very much no matter what happens. As he began to calm down, the baby started crying and reaching for the mother. She said, "Leelee is going to have to wait while I cuddle Tommy." Tommy smiled through his tears and began to snuggle against his mother, who was joking about Leelee being a little hog. Tommy laughed, relaxed in his mother's arms, and took full advantage of his chance to have his mother's undivided attention. Then he said, "Tommy is a Mommy hog." Afterward, Tommy was able for the rest of the day to share better spontaneously, to refrain from dangerous aggression, and to express unhappiness in words. The message conveyed in his mother's session with him was, "I love you no matter what. I understand your feelings. You can tell them to me, but you cannot hurt the baby. We can hold instead. I will try to give you more of my attention." This is a very different approach from just stopping Tommy from hurting the baby. By itself, the necessarily sharp intervention lowers the child's self-esteem without making better contact, when the need for contact was the cause of the misbehavior in the first place. *Holding time* ensures adequate contact while it sets a limit on behavior.

Sometimes sibling rivalry is expressed indirectly. Ned was a seemingly happy, well-adjusted three-year-old until his baby brother was born. Although he expressed a hope that the baby wasn't staying long, he accepted him and behaved in a protective way. For instance, one day when the baby cried, Ned picked him up and carried him to his mother. At the same time, he was showing extreme aggression toward the parents. Ned's anger seemed better placed than Tommy's attacks on the baby, but his parents were also distressed. Then the mother began regular *holding* with Ned. After a couple of weeks, instead of being aggressive, Ned began to ask for *holding* when he felt upset.

Contrary to advice sometimes offered, it is important not to ignore bickering, tattling, or aggression. These are not just manipulation but symptoms of unmet needs for love and attention. They are not useful exercises in conflict resolution but signs of a child out of control. They are both causes and effects of low self-esteem.

In addition to *holding*, it does help to make rules and state guidelines. Even very young children can participate in rule making. They can also help think of reasonable consequences of misbehavior. Just stating the rules will not control behavior, but if they are in good contact with you, your children will want to follow the rules to please you. Then as they develop, they will internalize the rules and treat them as their own. Without the good connection to you, they will not have the incentive to follow the rules. Punishment is not as successful a deterrent as love and attention are an incentive. *Holding time* is a better way to make a good connection.

Parents often try to give each child an equal share of the pie. This is a mistake. You should give each child what he needs. If Johnny gets a pair of boots when his brother Jimmy doesn't need boots, don't buy boots or anything else for Jimmy. If Jimmy complains, realize that he needs more of you, not an equal share of boots. If Julie is sick and takes extra attention, you should hold her brother Bobby to help him deal with his feelings about the decrease in attention from you during his sister's illness. You may not be able to give him an equal share of attention, but you can listen to, understand, and show empathy for his feelings. He will not feel cheated if his feelings are accepted. He will even help you take care of Julie.

The benefit to you will be a harmonious family. Sibling squabbling is one of the most nerve-wracking situations in parenting. *Holding time* will spare you that distress.

If you show preference for one child, both children will feel threatened. Obviously it will affect the self-esteem of the underdog, because he won't feel as highly valued and loved. But the preferred child will be hurt as well, because he will worry about keeping your love. If you prefer him, there must not be enough love for both. Also, preferred children often feel pressured to perform in order to keep your love. They do not feel accepted for themselves but rather for what they can do. They want unconditional love as much as the other sibling does. If you prefer one child, it is a sign of your lack of connection with the other. *Holding time* will help you to solidify your connection with both, and you will be able to value and praise each as an individual.

Children are quick to make comparisons themselves, calling to your attention every imagined inequality in treatment. Parents put themselves in an untenable position when they try to make everything equal. It is impossible to equalize either attention or possessions. It is far better to meet each child's needs individually. Jan, a well-adjusted eight-year-old, asked for a new coat when her sister got one. Their mother said, "Jan, I will buy you a new coat when you outgrow your blue coat." Jan knew she didn't need a new coat and was reasonably satisfied with the answer.

Six-year-old Annie asked for a new dress when her sister got one. When their mother said she didn't need one, Annie began to fuss. No explanation satisfied her. She cried and fussed all the way home, and her fussing escalated into a temper tantrum. Out of desperation, her mother began *holding*. Annie's feelings of unworthiness came out, along with her perception that her mother preferred her twelve-year-old sister Susie because she was buying her so many new clothes lately. Mother explained that Susie had had a growth spurt and could not fit into her old clothes. She told Annie how much she loved her and her sister as well. She told her how hurt and sad she was to hear Annie's distress. She even cried a little. Annie was touched by her mother's expression of feelings. They hugged and looked into each

Sarah's turn.

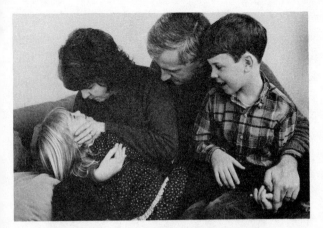

*She doesn't
want holding.
John is gleeful.*

*She sticks
out her tongue
in defiance.*

*She cries and
screams.*

She rejects her mother.

Once her angry feelings are gone, she calms down.

She makes direct and willing contact.

202

Joyfully she trades kisses with Mom.

Sarah is ready to talk with Mom.

Sarah showers affection on Dad too.

203

John reaches out to Sarah.

*Sarah is
flooded with
positive feelings.*

other's eyes. Annie said, "Thanks for standing my anger, Mommy. I love you." During the *holding time,* her mother realized that she had not been paying as much attention to Annie as usual because of Susie's need for extra attention. She promised to spend extra time with Annie. It was clear the dress was not the real issue.

Children with a handicapped sibling deserve special mention. No matter how hard a parent tries to keep the normal child from being adversely affected, that child will suffer in some ways. The handicapped child simply takes extra attention. It is impossible for the normal sibling to avoid some feelings of jealousy about the extra care, rage about his own unmet needs, and then guilt for having the jealousy and rage. A parent can help by understanding these feelings, by discussing them, and by showing the child that the feelings do not make the child unacceptable or unlovable. Of course, the child is not allowed to *act* on the rage and jealousy. Feelings can be discussed at any time, and they can be discussed and vented during *holding.* The handicapped child can be helped to deal with the same feelings: jealousy of the sibling for being normal, rage at his own helplessness, and guilt about his negative feelings and for causing so much trouble. There is no better gift from parent to child than the security the child feels from being loved and accepted, feelings and all.

Children with an outstanding sibling also have an extra burden. There is a problem when athletic or intellectual abilities are unequal or when one child is physically more attractive. Short boys with tall sisters often have special difficulties, as does an older child whose slightly younger sibling is bigger or smarter. Parents can offset some of the child's distress by giving him a close and gratifying relationship with them. A child develops high self-esteem when he knows he is loved unconditionally. He will place high value on relationships, and his enjoyment of life and sense of self will come from his ability to connect with people. He doesn't have to be exceptional to connect. In fact, exceptional children often have more difficulties relating to others because they are more sensitive and are bombarded by more stimuli. If you have an exceptional child, you will need to establish a close and effective bond as a protection from oversensitivity. *Holding time,* by ensuring a good connection, helps both the normal child and the exceptional sibling.

Twins create a special dilemma because it is difficult to give adequate care and attention to two babies at once. Acknowledging the disadvantages, you can work to offset them. This system is a lifesaver because it provides a shortcut to close attachment, and you certainly need shortcuts with twins. One pitfall is to let twins take care of each other. They often ask less of the parents because they have each other. Try to give each child as much undivided attention as possible. Try to discover their differences. If you are well connected to each one, you will be sensitive to each one's needs and be able to respond to them. As with other children, if twins vie for attention, recognition, or possessions, it is a clear sign that they need *holding time.*

While twins are an obvious problem, children born less than eighteen months apart pose a problem that often goes unrecognized. When the tiny new baby comes, the older child seems like a giant and is often treated like one. It is a temptation to push the older one toward self-sufficiency as soon as the second pregnancy announces itself. In reality, he is still a baby with enormous needs. If he does not receive the attention and nurturing he needs once the new baby arrives, the result will be intense rivalry or even depression. Parents who are aware of this dilemma in advance can do a great deal to prevent the older child from feeling pushed out. *Holding* is a good way to reassure the child that he is still loved, still your baby, and still being nurtured. It is a time when he can voice his feelings about sharing you and you can show that you accept his feelings. Sharing ceases to be a problem when a child is secure in your love and attention. When you meet your child's needs, you are giving him a chance for optimal development as a healthy competitor in a competitive world.

PART FOUR

Holding Time Works: How Are You Doing?

15.

ISSUES AND ANSWERS

Questions Everyone Asks

About Holding Time

There are many questions that arise when mothers think about integrating *holding time* into their family life. Probably you already have some.

How do I find time when I am already stretched as far as I can go?

This is a natural worry. However, you will quickly discover that *holding time* is a shortcut, not a burden. But there will only be time if you make a firm decision to make time. Imagine that your life and your child's life depend on it. In a way this is true, because without *holding time* your attachment with your child is constantly threatened by the complexities of daily life. You must carve out time for this crucial activity. The ideal way to ensure that you will find time is to resolve to do it daily. If you say you will do it four times a week, you may find yourself putting it off to the next day. Alternatively, if you make a regular schedule, you will rarely need to have an emergency session. Your child will be in such good contact with you that he will generally behave well and communicate openly with you.

The other way to schedule it is to make a decision to do it each time there is a sign that your child needs it. The drawback to doing it only when it is absolutely necessary is that the behavior is apt to occur at times when *holding* is very inconvenient if not impossible. Also, if you do it on a regular schedule you can be more certain of having the time to complete the full cycle.

Of course, the ideal is to use *holding time* both ways. Schedule a regular time each day, and do it again if your child's behavior indicates a need. When you schedule it regularly each day, it does not have to be at the same hour. Every day can be different. But if you schedule it at some specific time, it may be easier.

The other advantage of doing it on a regular schedule is that children save up their distress for their *holding time* if they know for sure that they will have one. Also, if they know they will have one at some point, they can be patient while you hold a sibling. If a child doesn't feel certain of having his turn, he will interfere when you are doing *holding* with his sister or brother. One of the most touching examples of a child's ability to wait for his turn was Mike, age four, who ran to his mother after being hit on the head with a block by his two-year-old sister. Instead of blaming her or asking for attention for himself, he said, "Mommy, Christine hit me. She needs holding." Then he waited by his mother's side until she finished with Christine so he could have his own turn.

How long does it go on?
Each session can last up to about one hour at first. Experienced mother-child pairs who do it regularly if not daily report that they can go through all the phases in a few minutes. The length of each session is dependent on many factors, including

how long it has been since the last session, what problems have arisen in your lives in the interim, what prompted this particular *holding*, and how well you release and communicate your own feelings.

Do I go on using holding time *indefinitely, and if not, when do I stop?*

Children often make their mothers promise never to stop doing it. Once they experience the joy of open communication that this method gives them, they want to make sure that they will always have it. Whenever you stop, you will know that you always have it available for use with your child if you need it to strengthen your attachment.

An example of parents who used *holding time* with their children and still do now that the children have children of their own is Paula and Carl. They started holding all of their children when their youngest had some developmental problems. Now that two of the daughters have their own children, they are using the technique too. There have been a number of severe problems in this family, but everyone has remained close and helpful to each other. They have used *holding* in times of crisis but not regularly. Each family can find out for itself how to make the best use.

Will holding time *cause my child to be overly dependent on me? What if I die?*

I am always surprised by this question and worry that many mothers may be inhibiting a strong attachment with their children for fear of harming them if they should die. Just the opposite is to be feared: if you have a weak attachment with your child, he will do poorly if you die. If he has a strong attachment, he will be insulated against the devastation of losing you. How is this possible? If you provide your child with a strong bond, he will have more self-confidence, higher self-esteem, and greater motivation to launch out into the world. He will have known what it is to have a mutually gratifying relationship. He will want to and will know how to establish a similar relationship with other people. His chances of finding a good mother-substitute will be enhanced. His chances of finding a good spouse in later life will also be greater.

The notion that your child will become too dependent on you is not supported by experience. On the contrary, it appears that children of all ages become more independent, more self-reliant, and more self-confident through strong attachment. *Holding time* does not create dependence. If your child starts clinging when you've begun *holding,* it will be because the dependency was already there. *Holding time* makes you aware of existing problems. Fortunately, it solves the problems as it uncovers them. What it does create is the capacity for *interdependence.* Interdependence calls for sensitivity to one's own and to the other person's needs and feelings, the desire and effort to be responsive to the needs of the other, the desire and the ability to communicate openly about feelings and thoughts with that person, and the capacity to enjoy spending time together.

The extent to which children can engage in a mutually gratifying relationship is impressive. When their needs are met, they are ready to meet other people's needs. For this reason it is a rewarding experience to be with a child whose needs have been filled.

Will holding a child against his will break his spirit?

Children really want to be held, as you will discover. They fight you because it helps them deal with their feelings. As one child said, "It helps me get my angries out." A child may give a thousand good reasons why you shouldn't hold him, and then turn around and say, "Can we do this again tomorrow?" My own son at age seven always said he hated *holding* before we started a session, only to give me subsequently a proposed schedule of *holding* for the rest of the week.

The best statement from a child endorsing *holding time* is the answer to the question, "How do you feel afterward?" You will hear, "I feel as though I have never been angry and never will be." It does not break a child's spirit; rather it frees his spirit from the burden of anger and other negative feelings which interfere with his self-expression and fulfillment.

How can I be confident that a child wants to be held when the child denies it adamantly?

It is very difficult at times to believe that your child really wants to be held, because of the intense resistance and rejection. Common complaints that really hurt a mother relate to the mother's smell: "You stink." "I can't stand the way you smell." "You have bad breath." "You have B.O." "I can't breathe." It is fascinating to see these very personal insults change to their opposites. At least half the children I have seen in *holding time,* whether two years old or ten, comment about disliking their mother's scent, only to tell her later that they love it.

Another common set of complaints goes like this: "Where have you been?" "You're never there." "You don't deserve a hug." "Why should I do this when you want to?" The implied criticism in these complaints is that the mother has not been reliable in meeting the child's needs. The child is saying, "You have not been available to me, so why should I be available to you?" This situation is the opposite of a mutually gratifying interdependent relationship. Without *holding time,* a mother and child might get into a retaliatory scenario, because no mother can feel positively toward her child when rejected. And if you are the mother of a preverbal baby, remember that the baby's rejection can be just as strong and just as personal without words.

Instead of judging whether or not your child really wants to be held on the basis of the nature and quantity of the rejection he unleashes on you during the *holding,* judge on the basis of his subsequent behavior generally and interaction with you specifically. Mothers who have done *holding time* with their children report no ill effects. Even the incomplete sessions usually yield some observable positive result.

Does there have to be an angry phase every time?

Not always. Sometimes another emotion is the main focus, such as hurt or sadness or jealousy or fear. But most mothers report that some angry feelings bother a child every day. The majority of mothers have discovered that if they do not elicit negative feelings every day, these usually will pop up in some undesirable behavior. The mother of three-year-old Mary reported, "I was not doing it daily. I found I reached a plateau where I couldn't go any further. Mary said she was afraid to express her anger. Recently, I started holding her almost daily and wondering sometimes, 'Am I creating more anger?' But what she says is, 'I *like* all this holding.' Then she gives me the feedback which tells me it's the right thing."

Another example of the need for giving the child's anger an outlet is Lisa, an eleven-year-old who had been enjoying daily *holding.* On a holiday she and her mother had a whole day together: shopping, lunch out, a shower together, cooking, reading at bedtime. Lisa started to cry when it was time for lights out. She asked her mother why they hadn't had *holding time.* Her mother had felt so content with their day and so sublimely connected that she was shocked to hear that Lisa still wanted it. Lisa explained that *holding time* gave her a release of upset and a closeness she could not get any other way.

It is probably very beneficial to allow for all the phases on a daily basis. But every little bit seems to count a great deal, so don't be discouraged if you don't do a complete cycle every day. On the other hand, expect to see anger come out in some manner. *Holding time* provides a circumscribed way in which the child can release his feelings and at the same time not feel guilty about them or worry about his mother's anger when she reciprocates with release of her feelings. *Holding time* is prevention. If a child can't be certain that he will have one, he will not be able to save his distress. Therefore, if you know you cannot do it on a given day, tell him. Make a date with him for a day when you will surely do it. In the meantime, if your child fails to save his distress, explain to him that you can understand why the anger or hurt is coming out now and that you will talk about it during the next session. He will be grateful for your understanding, and it may enable him to stop acting out his distress. If he remains out of control, you may have to hold, if only briefly. This is not a punishment but an attempt to restore his equilibrium and yours as well.

How will holding time *be accepted by my husband?*

This description of the results was given by a father who was very skeptical at first: "I'm not there for most of the *holding,* but I can tell by the way my daughter's behaving when she hasn't had enough. You really can read it. But, I'll tell you, listening to it is horrifying. The first time I heard my daughter scream I wanted to go rip her out of my wife's arms and take her away for the rest of her life, but I learned it's a definitely worthwhile technique. My daughter is just a regular kid, but it really has helped her. It, in turn, has helped us."

This last sentence is one key to fathers' attitudes. If it helps mother and child, it helps father and mother, and father and child as well.

Another father was kept away from home until all hours working. However, after *holding time* had brought peace to his family, he began to appear at home for dinner or even earlier. Eventually he participated in it with his wife and the children.

When the mother attains a better relationship with her child, the father can then start to have his own *holding time* with the child too. It is easier for mothers to do *holding* than to listen or watch or even to participate as a support to someone else. Many fathers also find it difficult at first to help their wives do the *holding,* but they find it even more difficult to do it themselves. After watching the mother a few times, fathers usually feel more comfortable about it. Luckily, there is plenty of time. Be patient and let it happen naturally.

What should we talk about during holding time?

This problem takes care of itself when you let the child express his feelings. If you deal with the issues that arise, you will have plenty to talk about. Be sure to share your own feelings with your child. You are allowed, of course, to bring up things that have been bothering you too. But remember that you can just hold without talking. As long as you allow your child to battle through the rejection phase and join together with you in the resolution, you will be doing *holding time* correctly.

What do I do about violence?

Children often try to bite or pinch or pull their mother's hair. Do not allow your child to hurt you. It is not good for him. It will scare him. It will make him feel terrible about himself. Tell him that he is not allowed to hurt you. Then physically stop him from hurting you when he tries. Do what you must to stop him. Change your position. Mothers who are trying to restrain a very aggressive child find lying down to be the best position. They can use their bodies to keep the child from hurting them. Two hands are not always enough.

Can holding time *substitute for punishment?*

If you use *holding time* regularly, chances are you won't have much need for punishment. Children who are acting in a way that calls for punishment are out of touch with you. This method brings them back into positive contact with you. If you see bad behavior, think of restoring contact. If you cannot do it otherwise, use *holding time.* It is a fail-safe way to make contact.

The main principle is to refuse to accept bad behavior. You can't tolerate unacceptable behavior just because a child is angry. Children can channel their anger. They can tell you about it. They can ask for *holding*. They should not be allowed to *act* on anger.

At what age do I start holding time?
The ideal time to start holding is, of course, at birth. Carry the baby in a front pack. Sleep with your baby. Have as much contact as you can. If your baby becomes upset, hold him until he is calm and happy. If your child is older, begin now. Babies and children need to be able to take comfort from you. *Holding time* will enable the baby or child to turn to you for comfort even if you are the cause of the distress.

How do I do holding time *that first time? Do I explain what I am doing, or do I just begin?*
Either works. If you feel better explaining your actions, give the child a very brief description of the process. An example is: "I have wanted to be closer with you than we have been lately. I want to hold you now until we both feel good." Then do it. Do not wait for your child's approval. Just do it.

You can hold silently through all the phases, or you can talk when you feel like it. If your child talks, respond to what he is saying in a feeling way. It is sometimes useful to talk about how you felt about holding your child when he was a baby and how you have missed that feeling. He has missed it too. Or you can begin by explaining what about your relationship has hurt, upset, or angered you.

The main task is to begin. The three phases happen automatically. One mother reported feeling very resistant to the idea of *holding time*. At the same time she felt that she really needed to do something with her five-year-old, whose behavior was quite disagreeable. Once she began, her son, Andy, did not give her much of a struggle, but they did go through all three phases. At the end Andy revealed to his mother that he did not like to be put in his room as a punishment. She asked what to do instead. He suggested being put "on the sofa to sit quietly without being isolated." Then he complained that his father didn't hold him while watching TV anymore. His mother promised she would tell Daddy to hold him. After this session Andy's behavior improved dramatically. His mom had started *holding time* reluctantly but felt so encouraged by the result that doing it a second time did not worry her at all.

Is it easier to begin when I am angry at a specific behavior?
In some ways it is easier to do it when you are provoked. Certainly no explanation is necessary for grabbing a misbehaving child. He already knew how you would feel about his misbehavior. He may be surprised to find himself being held, but he will not be surprised that you are reacting to his behavior. Mothers who have been apprehensive about "stirring up trouble" by starting to hold will find that during a tantrum is an excellent time to begin. The child is out of control, and you are not in control. So you have nothing to lose. Grab him and hang on tightly.

How can I do holding time *on a daily basis with more than one child?*
It may not be possible to do it every day with each of your children. You have to fit it in when you can. One mother found it so helpful with her three children that she felt compelled to find time for three sessions a day. She did one child before breakfast, one before dinner, and one after. Another mother with six children decided to hold ten minutes with each child daily and do a full, three-phase *holding* when she could. She felt that she got such good results that she continued this pattern. Each of you can experiment until you find a schedule that works for you and your family.

Should fathers do regular holding time *as well?*
This is another issue that each family has to work out individually. The only caution I would give is that a father's *holding* is

not a substitute for a mother's. Problems will arise in the mother-father-child relationship if the father does it instead of the mother. The father must be careful to support the mother-child relationship. If he interposes himself between mother and child, they will both feel threatened. Fathers' *holding* works best in a family in which the mother and father have a close, comfortable relationship and work well together as parents. However, mothers report that the most helpful practice is for the father to sometimes hold mother and child together.

What about sexuality?
Parents fear that close physical holding will be sexually stimulating to children. The increase in awareness of sexual abuse and incest has led to further worry. In practice, it appears that the children do not experience physical closeness as a sexual interaction. Sexuality seems to be more of a concern to parents than to children. The worry is quickly dispelled when they actually practice *holding time*. They discover that the kind of closeness they attain is not at all of a sexual nature. In fact, the open communication promoted by this technique ensures against the very kind of secrecy and manipulation involved in sexual abuse of children.

Of course, mother-child intimacy includes physical as well as mental and spiritual closeness. Mother and child should continue to be physically affectionate and expressive throughout the developmental years. When things go right, both take pleasure in physical affection. This pleasure is not sexual. Too often both parents back away from their child's physical approaches for fear of sexual overtones. It is particularly important to maintain physical closeness with children as they approach and enter adolescence. If they are hungry for affection, they are more likely to become involved in sexual activity before they should.

Fathers are more apt to withdraw than mothers. Fathers, do not withdraw! Hug your girls. Hug your boys. They need your physical expression of caring.

Many mothers have reluctantly admitted to feelings of sensual pleasure from closeness with babies, especially from nursing. When they discover that this is natural and necessary for the survival of the species, they are relieved and freer to luxuriate in the pleasure of physical affection throughout their child's development.

Which child do I choose first in beginning holding time?

It is ironic that the child the mother thinks will be her easiest is often her most difficult. It is not clear why this is so commonly true. In some cases, I think the chosen child is the one the mother feels is easiest for her to handle in general. When she begins *holding,* she discovers that the child has a buildup of anger because he has been "good" despite his angry feelings. Don't worry. You will not make the child's behavior worse. He will be happier because he will no longer carry this burden. Try to permit his expression of feeling and try to understand and accept it. Once you accept the feelings, you will come together in a peaceful resolution. You will see his relief and probably his gratitude for the unconditional love that you have just succeeded in giving him by holding on throughout his anger. Your "good" or "easy" child will be even better and easier; he will be even more responsive to your needs and wishes because his actions will no longer be at his own expense.

In any case, it doesn't really matter which child you choose to begin with. Just be sure to do all of your children as soon as you are able. Whenever you begin, tell all of them they will each have a turn.

Isn't bringing out a child's distress just looking for trouble?

Holding time does not just stir things up. A child's distress is acted out in many ways. Facing it head-on can lead to a true resolution of the conflict. If the child's feelings do not come out, you should try to guess what they might be. If your guess doesn't hit the mark, the child will dismiss it. A child will not adopt a feeling that you have suggested unless it rings true. Until you help him think about them, a child often does not realize what his feelings are. He will let a wrong guess pass and wait for you to hit the mark. The important principle is to keep trying.

When I use holding time *in response to a tantrum, am I not rewarding bad behavior?*

One of the most important applications is dealing with tantrums. Tantrums make a parent feel helpless and even desperate. A child out of control is frightening. Most parents also become enraged. This often leads to poor child management at the moment of the tantrum. *Holding time* gives the parents a safe and loving way of handling this emotional emergency. It saves the parent from saying or doing things that make the situation worse. It gives them both an outlet for their upset. Beyond these momentary controls, it brings the parent into loving contact with the child. The underlying cause of the tantrum is that the child is out of contact. Both parent and child learn a more positive way of handling distress. Furthermore, regular *holding* eliminates bad behavior because even children as young as toddlers learn to save their anger. It does not reward bad behavior. It usually prevents it.

If you only use *holding time* for one situation, let it be to handle tantrums. Toddlers are famous for tantrums, but they do appear in all age groups. The minute a tantrum starts, grab your child wherever you are. Hold on. You will be putting yourself back in charge. You will not suffer the feelings of helplessness that overcome a parent during a child's tantrum. You will be setting a firm but loving limit on his behavior. Children interpret such limits as a sign of love and caring, even if they resist and protest. *Holding time* gives you a way of becoming close just when you both feel very distant.

Should I try to form a support group for holding time?

Many mothers just start doing it alone for practical reasons.

But some mothers do like the reinforcement a group provides. In fact, the first few mothers to learn about it as a way of maintaining close family ties felt that a group in which to do it would ensure that they continue. They started a mothers' group, which met weekly. One hour was devoted to mother-child *holding*. The second hour was for socializing and discussing issues that arose from this and from other family experiences. The group met in a local church, and anyone could drop in. Other smaller, less organized groups of mothers have met regularly and some only from time to time. In some cases two mothers have made a date for regular sessions, taking turns meeting at each other's houses. Such meetings help the mothers, and often the kids like them too. Some kids don't; they prefer privacy. The groups are mostly for the benefit of the mothers, and they must decide which way to go. The important point is to do *holding* regularly, whether alone or in a group.

If I have no special problems with my children, should I still do holding time?

Parents can readily imagine specific applications, especially when problems arise with their child. It is harder to imagine doing it when there are no obvious conflicts. I have tried to show that there is great value in the close attachment it engenders and also that it solves very specific problems. You will decide from experience whether you make it an established routine or use it to attack problems after they arise.

What happens if I stop doing holding time?

If you do *holding time* for a while, you will enjoy a closer, easier relationship with your child that will not disappear if you stop. Most mothers have found that they can maintain better contact if they use it regularly. Sometimes children ask for more if their mothers stop. Sometimes bad behavior reminds a mother she has stopped!

What happens if I don't achieve a good resolution?

You can fail to reach a resolution for a variety of reasons, the most common being an unavoidable interruption by some pressing event. But another reason can be that you are not expressing *your* feelings of hurt or anger. Often a child will not give in until the mother responds to the rejection. Many times even when a resolution is not reached, the child feels better anyway.

Why does my child seem happy after holding time, *while I still feel terrible?*

After a complete resolution, both mother and child usually feel wonderful. If you still feel terrible, it means you did not reach a true resolution. This is not bad; your child's behavior is probably obviously better, and he is more responsive to you. If neither of you seems to be better, try to hold on longer. Continue until you are melting into each other's bodies in a mutually satisfying cuddle. Look into each other's eyes and tell each other how you feel. You may provoke a new rejection phase trying to make eye contact. Go through the cycle again until you finally reach a resolution. You will know it by your good feelings.

Do most mothers reach a resolution on the first try?

Some do. Some don't. The more determined the mother is at the outset, the faster she seems to reach a resolution. If you don't do it in the first session, try harder the next time. Don't give up even if it takes several tries; the results are worth it.

How do I keep from becoming discouraged when my child won't give in to a resolution?

Often a child will not give in until his mother has exposed the depths of her feelings of hurt, anger, rejection, and frustration. Talk about your feelings. Show your feelings. You will probably cry. Go ahead.

Insist on eye contact. If you don't get it, you are still in a partial or full rejection. Fight for complete eye contact. Explain how you feel when you don't have it. Insist on being hugged and cuddled. It is not enough for your child just to allow himself to be held by you. If he doesn't snuggle into you, you are still in the rejection phase. Don't give up until *you* feel better. When your child reaches a resolution, you will feel better.

Do some mothers give up altogether?
Some mothers do give up. Usually some situation occurs later which makes them feel so desperate that they try once again. Then they may continue on a regular basis. Others go on without it until they are desperate again.

Isn't the initial confrontation similar to resolution?
Confrontation can at first feel similar to a resolution. You both settle into a phase of tuning in to your own thoughts. As you each allow yourself to recognize your own feelings, you begin to realize both your good and bad feelings. Usually a child begins to fight to escape from *holding* to avoid the distress. This fight becomes the rejection phase. The child may go back and forth between rejection and resolution. The repeated transitions can feel similar to the initial transition from confrontation to resolution. However, when a final resolution is reached, the hurt, anger, and upset are gone. Mother and child are really tuned in to each other in a free and positive way that lasts. Then continued holding *does not rekindle a rejection phase.*

What if holding *doesn't proceed in three phases as described?*
There are many variations in the pattern, as I have just described. Sometimes *holding* begins with rejection right away, especially with an experienced child. Sometimes it goes from rejection to a partial resolution and then back to a rejection. If the mother persists, the rejection usually reaches a peak, a catharsis occurs, and the final resolution follows. A child may occasionally fall asleep during the rejection phase and then

wake up resolved, but the child may also wake up fighting. No two pairs will have quite the same experiences, and no two sessions will be identical. Your goal is to be flexible but to hang on until you reach a better communication and closeness.

What phase of holding time *is most helpful?*

All parts seem to be helpful to a child, and all convey a message of unconditional love: "I will hold you no matter how you feel or what you say." When a mother holds on throughout the rejection phase, a child gains a great sense of security. He learns that, with all of his feelings, he is acceptable. The mother learns that she can tolerate her child's feelings of distress as well as her own. Both learn that anger will not be allowed to come between them. They can share pain. Then during the resolution they learn to share the whole range of good feelings. Because the bad feelings are tolerable, they are free to share their yearnings for closeness and to be close.

Is it possible that neither person is storing anger or distress?

Yes. When there are no negative feelings, a mother and child can go from confrontation straight to resolution. It happens sometimes when a pair has been doing *holding time* regularly with successful resolutions. Sometimes just discussing a problem will lead to a resolution. Resolution without rejection is not too common because daily life is full of upsets.

Should I hold a sick child?

When a child is ill, simple cuddling as opposed to *holding* is often the best option. Usually children readily accept cuddling when they don't feel well. Since their barriers are down, you have easy access to closeness, which is after all the object of *holding time.* Going through a rejection phase may be too much; if a child is congested, you don't want crying. If a child has an ear infection or an earache, don't do *holding.*

Should I hold my emotionally disturbed child?
Holding time does help disturbed children. However, with severely disturbed children, professional consultation is advisable. In some cases *holding time* could be incorporated into the therapy.

Can holding time *stop bed-wetting?*
Yes, it has stopped bed-wetting in some cases. Approximately one million children in the United States suffer from this problem, yet only 14 percent of bed wetters ages five to nine outgrow it annually if untreated. Some bed wetters have physical abnormalities, which must be handled medically. However, a large percentage are merely so deeply asleep that they are not aware of the sensation of a full bladder. I postulate that *holding time* establishes a balance between two biological systems, adrenaline and the endorphins. The balance is known to regulate the level of arousal. *Holding time* may help children maintain a better pattern of arousal during both waking and sleeping. In my experience, bed-wetting often ceases after four to six weeks of daily *holding*. A second benefit in cases of bed-wetting is that the mother can channel her frustration into the *holding* experience instead of making the situation worse by yelling or by criticizing the child. As a result, the mother and child do not experience a rift. They feel empathy for each other rather than anger, hurt, or frustration.

If one of my children hurts the other, which should I hold first?
It is best to hold the aggressor first, because he is out of control. *Holding time* will put you back in charge of him and help him to regain his control. Then you can hold the injured party for comfort. The injured party may not be innocent in the sibling conflict. This question will emerge and can be dealt with.

What if one child doesn't stick up for himself?
Some children are less feisty. Some have made a correct as-

sessment that they can't win against a particular aggressor. You will find out during *holding* what is behind your child's passivity. If it is lack of confidence, he will begin to gain it through the closeness and security of *holding.*

The behavior of my only child resembles sibling rivalry. What can this mean?
An only child can exhibit rivalry. It could be with other children, with one parent for the other parent's love, or with a parent for a grandparent's love. As with any child, it is a sign of low self-esteem and strained mother-child attachment. The remedy is the same as for sibling rivalry, that is to say, a better attachment with the mother.

How can I teach my child to share?
When a child feels secure in your love, he is generous with his love and with his possessions. Try not to force a child to share. Set a good example and be sure you give enough love and attention. If he becomes involved in a tussle over sharing and it is a significant issue, use *holding* to allow him to vent his frustrations. Be sympathetic but don't force him to share.

Should I hold my kids when they are screaming at each other?
Yes. They are out of control. You will reestablish control and deal with their upset feelings at the same time.

How can I stop my children from denigrating each other?
Abuse, whether verbal or physical, is out-of-control behavior. During *holding,* tell each child how painful it is to see this kind of interaction. Tell them how you want them to act toward each other, and ask each to imagine how the other feels about being abused. Try to give more attention to each.

When my two children fight over toys, should I help them work it out?
Stepping in rarely works in any long-range way, but not inter-

vening doesn't work either. Parents don't want to be around squabbling children, even if it doesn't seem to harm the children. If for no other reason than to make a peaceful setting for parents and children together, squabbling should be handled. It is not a useful mode of communication, and it is another sign of being out of control. You can teach them a better way by example, and you can let them vent their feelings in *holding,* but don't let them fight. Parents who do regular *holding time* report new levels of harmony.

Why does my children's tattling on each other drive me to distraction?

This is another form of sibling rivalry; they are attempting to win your attention, but tattling is a negative way to ask for it. *Holding* will give you a constructive outlet for your anger and will provide a way of giving your children the needed attention.

When my kids fight over space in my lap, refusing to share it, should I do holding time?

Whether children vie for possessions, recognition, or attention, it is a sign that they feel their needs are not met well enough. You want them to realize that you have enough love for both of them. They are afraid you don't. *Holding* will show them that you love them despite their seemingly selfish needs, their jealousy, their anger, fear, or rivalry. They will feel secure in your love and feel good about themselves. Security and self-esteem help eliminate sibling rivalry. Instead of enemies you will see two children who are free to enjoy and love each other, and you will enjoy two children who can love you in return.

Is holding time some sort of panacea?

It is a solution for problems that stem from strained attachments. Much of the difficult behavior of children has been accepted as normal because it is so common. *Holding time* has enlightened us by showing that well-attached children are freer of difficult behavior than we had thought possible. Furthermore, the increased strength of the bond leads parents to appropriate expectations not too high, not too low—a key to a child's good self-image and positive attitude toward life.

However, there are some important concepts which should be added to *holding*: good nutrition, adequate rest, appropriate kinds and amounts of exercise, time for play and fun, especially as a family, and reading together. Perhaps most important of all is a good example from parents.

16.

NOW THAT I'M HOLDING,
AM I DOING IT RIGHT?

The Checklists

This chapter contains a checklist that has been designed to help you measure your results with *holding time.* Your scores will help you establish a baseline before you begin and then a new level after you have had experience. The scores will be relative results: they are not meant to be compared with those of other people but rather are to chart your progress. If you do *holding time* as it is set forth in this book, your scores will rise over time.

As you use this method regularly, your ability to cope will improve, your child's behavior will improve, and of course you will know it. The checklist is meant only to be a yardstick to indicate to you where you started and how far you have progressed. Perhaps most important, the questions themselves will help alert you to your need for *holding time* for particular situations.

Part One should be answered before you begin using *holding time.*

If your score on Part One is 32–60, *holding time* is an emergency procedure for you because you are suffering needlessly.

If your score is 61–80, you could improve your situation considerably with *holding time.*

If your score is 81–90, keep up the good work and go for perfect with *holding time.*

After you have done several sessions, retake Part One. See if your score is rising. Then take Part Two. If your score on Part Two is 23–40, you are not using *holding time* enough. Reread Chapters 2 and 3.

If your score is 41–60, you are using *holding time* for many difficult interactions. No doubt you are having fewer such situations by now. Keep doing it and watch the scores rise.

HOW TO SCORE THE CHECKLISTS

Give your answers a point value.

PART ONE		PART TWO	
often	= 1	sometimes	= 1
sometimes	= 2	often	= 2
never	= 3	always	= 3

Count up the number of each answer. Multiply the number of each answer times the point value. For example, if you answered "sometimes" to twenty questions, then 20 x 2 = 40. If you answered "often" to three questions, 3 x 1 = 3. If you answered "never" nine times, then multiply 9 x 3 = 27. Add the total points 40 + 3 + 27 = 70. Your score for this part totals 70 points.

After using *holding time* regularly for a while, retake both parts. You should see a rising score. If your score does not rise, reread Chapter 3. Be sure to hold on until you reach a resolution. Then retake both parts and add the two scores. When you reach a combined score of 140, you will know you are doing adequate amounts and doing it right.

PART ONE: THE "WHO NEEDS *HOLDING TIME?*" CHECKLIST

SCORE:	1	2	3
1. When you are out of the house, do you wish you could stay away longer?	OFTEN ___	SOMETIMES ___	NEVER ___
2. When your child is difficult, do you wish someone else would take over the situation?	OFTEN ___	SOMETIMES ___	NEVER ___
3. Do you feel jealous when your child seems to prefer someone else to you?	OFTEN ___	SOMETIMES ___	NEVER ___
4. Do you find one of your children easier to deal with than another?	OFTEN ___	SOMETIMES ___	NEVER ___
5. Do you feel closer to one child than to another?	OFTEN ___	SOMETIMES ___	NEVER ___
6. Do you envy another mother's relationship with her child?	OFTEN ___	SOMETIMES ___	NEVER ___
7. Do you feel you are a better mother to one of your children than to another?	OFTEN ___	SOMETIMES ___	NEVER ___
8. Do you feel some mothers are better than you?	OFTEN ___	SOMETIMES ___	NEVER ___
9. Do you lose your temper with your child?	OFTEN ___	SOMETIMES ___	NEVER ___

10. Do you have to ask
your child more than once
to do things?   OFTEN ___   SOMETIMES ___   NEVER ___

11. Do you have to ask
your child more than once
to stop doing something? OFTEN ___   SOMETIMES ___   NEVER ___

12. Do you have to
threaten in order to
obtain results?   OFTEN ___   SOMETIMES ___   NEVER ___

13. Do you feel that you
have no time for yourself? OFTEN ___   SOMETIMES ___   NEVER ___

14. Do you feel that all
you do is give, give, give? OFTEN ___   SOMETIMES ___   NEVER ___

15. Do your children
fight?   OFTEN ___   SOMETIMES ___   NEVER ___

16. Does your child have
problems with peers?   OFTEN ___   SOMETIMES ___   NEVER ___

17. Does your child cling
to you?   OFTEN ___   SOMETIMES ___   NEVER ___

18. Is your child
extremely independent for
his/her age?   OFTEN ___   SOMETIMES ___   NEVER ___

19. Does your husband
disagree with your
handling of your child?   OFTEN ___   SOMETIMES ___   NEVER ___

20. Does your husband
contradict you with the
child?   OFTEN ___   SOMETIMES ___   NEVER ___

21. Are you annoyed with
your husband for not
doing his share of child
care?   OFTEN ___   SOMETIMES ___   NEVER ___

SCORE:	1	2	3
22. Are you embarrassed by your child's behavior in front of your friends or strangers?	OFTEN ___	SOMETIMES ___	NEVER ___
23. Does your child have difficulty adjusting to change?	OFTEN ___	SOMETIMES ___	NEVER ___
24. Is your child defiant?	OFTEN ___	SOMETIMES ___	NEVER ___
25. Does your child dawdle?	OFTEN ___	SOMETIMES ___	NEVER ___
26. Do you have trouble teaching your child to cooperate with household chores?	OFTEN ___	SOMETIMES ___	NEVER ___

TOTALS: ___   ___   ___

PART ONE TOTAL: _____

PART TWO: THE "NOW THAT I'M *HOLDING*, AM I DOING IT RIGHT?" CHECKLIST

SCORE:	1	2	3
1. Do you hold your child daily?	SOMETIMES ___	OFTEN ___	ALWAYS ___
2. Do you hold your child each time there is a difficulty between you?	SOMETIMES ___	OFTEN ___	ALWAYS ___

Do you hold your child when your child is . . .

	1	2	3
3. cranky?	SOMETIMES ___	OFTEN ___	ALWAYS ___

4. unreasonable? SOMETIMES ___ OFTEN ___ ALWAYS ___

5. provocative? SOMETIMES ___ OFTEN ___ ALWAYS ___

6. openly defiant? SOMETIMES ___ OFTEN ___ ALWAYS ___

7. stubborn? SOMETIMES ___ OFTEN ___ ALWAYS ___

8. dawdling? SOMETIMES ___ OFTEN ___ ALWAYS ___

9. negativistic? SOMETIMES ___ OFTEN ___ ALWAYS ___

10. argumentative? SOMETIMES ___ OFTEN ___ ALWAYS ___

11. disrespectful? SOMETIMES ___ OFTEN ___ ALWAYS ___

12. aggressive toward
others? SOMETIMES ___ OFTEN ___ ALWAYS ___

13. destructive? SOMETIMES ___ OFTEN ___ ALWAYS ___

14. withdrawn? SOMETIMES ___ OFTEN ___ ALWAYS ___

15. Do you use *holding*
when you formerly
would have sent your
child to his room? SOMETIMES ___ OFTEN ___ ALWAYS ___

16. Is your child more
physically affectionate
after *holding*? SOMETIMES ___ OFTEN ___ ALWAYS ___

17. Is your child more
verbally expressive to
you? SOMETIMES ___ OFTEN ___ ALWAYS ___

18. Does your child
have a greater capacity
to delay gratification? SOMETIMES ___ OFTEN ___ ALWAYS ___

19. Does your child
turn to you more for
support? SOMETIMES ___ OFTEN ___ ALWAYS ___

20. Does your child
have more self-
confidence? SOMETIMES ___ OFTEN ___ ALWAYS ___

SCORE:	1	2	3

21. Does your child have greater self-esteem?

SOMETIMES ___ OFTEN ___ ALWAYS ___

22. Does your child handle anger better?

SOMETIMES ___ OFTEN ___ ALWAYS ___

23. Do your children get along better with each other now?

SOMETIMES ___ OFTEN ___ ALWAYS ___

TOTALS: ___ ___ ___

PART TWO TOTAL: _____

PARTS ONE & TWO COMBINED SCORE: _____

AFTERWORD
Now Is the Time!

Now there is only one thing left for you to do. Hold. You are probably concerned about doing it right. Don't worry. Just begin. Your child will give you full credit for any and all attempts to be closer with him. If you will do it as it is outlined in this book, holding on until you reach a resolution each time, the results will speak for themselves.

To reach a resolution, it helps to follow these guidelines:

1. Help your child to get in touch with his feelings.

2. Accept his feelings.

3. Get in touch with your feelings and communicate them to your child.

4. Insist on eye contact.

5. Insist on being hugged and cuddled in return.

6. Keep holding until he feels better.

7. Keep holding until you feel better too.

Discovering *holding time* is like rediscovering the wheel. Once you are using it, it seems simple. In fact it is. It does take effort, but not as much effort as is demanded by the trouble you already have or will have with the everyday problems of child rearing.

We have been taught to accept some degree of frustration, anger, and aggression as normal in parent-child relationships. At the very least, the aggression is excessive and to a large degree unnecessary. An alternative for dramatic improvement exists. This alternative requires no financial expense, no ongoing visits to therapists, and in fact is totally under your control. *Holding time* is available to any mother who wishes to raise healthy, happy, successful children who are capable of loving others and of showing it. And in the process it will provide *you* with a more loving relationship with your children. The whole family can benefit, and you can get started right away. *Holding time* is now.

ACKNOWLEDGMENTS

It is with immeasurable gratitude that I acknowledge Nobel laureate Niko Tinbergen and his wife, Lies, who personally gathered a coterie of supporters from around the world for *holding time* and who wrote a book, as they said, to present the Welch method to therapists and parents.

Among the brilliant researchers whose work laid the foundation for my thinking are John Bowlby, D. W. Winnicott, Margaret Mahler, Marshall Klaus, John Kennell, James Robertson, Jane Goodall, Mary Ainsworth, Bessell Van der Kolk, and Ashley Montagu. I will always be in their debt.

Then there are the colleagues who aided my early work at Albert Einstein College of Medicine: Judith Vogel, Tamsin Looker, Leon Yorburg, Paul Low, Howard Owens, Hy Blank, Dave Mann, Byram Karasu, Robert Daly, the late Ed Sacher, and the late Marianne Kris. It was at Albert Einstein that I conceived of *holding time* as the key to strong mother-child attachment and first demonstrated that it led to optimal development.

Next there are the many professionals who have adopted the Welch method of holding and helped to spread its use throughout the world, most notably Jirina Prekop, Arno Gruen, Michele

Zappella, John Richer, Geraldine Flanagan, Anders Leissner, Leonie Fisher, George Victor, Rima Laibow, Joyce Forsythe, and Jo Stades-Veth. Their work has been of inestimable value.

Five other therapists deserve special mention for starting mothering centers modeled on mine: in England, Philippa Elmhirst, Jasmine Bailey, and Frankie Gardner; in Sweden, Christina Skogman; in Michigan, Patti Chaput. I admire their work, their courage, and their success.

I salute Dr. Henry Massie for undertaking a research project to study the effectiveness of Welch holding as a therapy for disturbed children.

In the preparation of *Holding Time* as in other aspects of my work, I have had the unfailing and indispensable encouragement and astute advice of my dear friend Zack Abuza, without whose direct help this book could not have been undertaken.

I owe more than I can say to my family: to my mother and father, Jane and Tom Welch, and my son, Bram, for their patience and love and continued full-time sacrifice and support, and for their direct participation in the work of this book and of the Mothering Center; and to my sister, Elizabeth Welch, M.D., and my brother-in-law, Stephen Glinick, M.D., for giving up their vacation time to help write and edit this book and for their special contribution resulting from using *holding time* with their daughter, Emily; and to my grandmother for the good mothering passed on to my mother and to me.

I am indebted to many other people as well who taught lessons that have been the guideposts of my work. First there are my patients and their families, whose love and humor and hurts and furies have given me special insights into the problems and rewards of human attachment. Next there is my brilliant and loving mentor, Matonah Rubin, who has been a wonderful model both as a psychiatrist and as a mother.

It is with warm feeling that I thank my friends who have sustained me and lovingly prodded me into completing this proj-

The author and her family, from left to right:
sister Beth with daughter, Emily;
mother, Jane; father, Tom; and son, Bram.

ect and continuing my work: Judith Vogel, Doug Moran, Janet Weisfogel, Aaron Beckwith, Bob Waggoner, Bea and Peter Crumbine, Elaine and Heinz Pagels, Ed Barber, and Dan Feld.

I give very special thanks to photojournalist Mary Ellen Mark for the generous contribution of her caring, talent, and time to create the wonderful photographs used throughout the book.

Special thanks too go to the families who allowed their holding sessions to be photographed for the book: Nicholas and Marilyn Harding; Sarah, John, Joan, and Paul Brixner; and Emily and Beth Welch Glinick.

I will be forever grateful to my editor at Simon and Schuster, Fred Hills, for his vision and enthusiasm in publishing *Holding Time*. His belief in me, his gentle encouragement, and his sensitive and creative editorial contribution have been invaluable.

SUGGESTED RESOURCES

BOOKS

1. Bowlby, John. *Attachment and Loss.* New York: Basic Books, 1980.

2. Flanagan, Geraldine. *The First Nine Months of Life.* New York: Simon and Schuster, 1962.

3. Fraiberg, Selma. *Every Child's Birthright. In Defense of Mothering.* New York: Basic Books, 1977.

4. Gallagher, Dorothy. *Hannah's Daughters. Six Generations of an American Family.* New York: Thomas Y. Crowell Co., 1976.

5. Giller, Robert and Matthews, Kathy. *Medical Makeover.* New York: Beech Tree Books. William Morrow, 1986.

6. Goodall, Jane. *In the Shadow of Man.* New York: Dell, 1971.

7. Heinl, Tina. *The Baby Massage Book. Using Touch for Better Bonding and Happier Babies.* Englewood Cliffs, New Jersey: Prentice-Hall, 1982.

8. Kavner, Richard S. *Your Child's Vision. A Parent's Guide to Seeing, Growing and Developing.* New York: Simon and Schuster, 1985.

9. Klaus, Marshall H. and Kennell, John H. *Mother-Infant Bonding.* St. Louis: C. V. Mosby, 1976.

10. Liedloff, Jean. *The Continuum Concept.* New York: Penguin Books, 1986.

11. Miller, Alice. *The Drama of the Gifted Child.* New York: Farrar, Straus and Giroux, 1983.

12. Montagu, Ashley. *Touching: The Human Significance of the Skin.* New York: Harper and Row, 1986.

13. Nilsson, Lennart. *A Child is Born.* New York: Delacorte Press, 1976.

14. Pryor, Karen. *Don't Shoot the Dog!* New York: Simon and Schuster, 1984.

15. Raphael, Dana. *The Tender Gift of Breastfeeding.* New York: Schocken Books, 1978.

16. Restak, Richard M. *The Infant Mind.* Garden City, New York: Doubleday, 1986.

17. Shainess, Natalie. *Sweet Suffering.* Indianapolis: Bobbs-Merrill, 1984.

18. Shedd, Charlie. *The Best Dad Is a Good Lover.* Kansas City: Sheed Andrews and McNeil, Subsidiary of Universal Press Syndicate, 1977.

19. Tattlebaum, Judy. *The Courage to Grieve.* New York: Harper & Row, 1980.

20. Thevenin, Tine. *The Family Bed. An Age-old Concept in Child Rearing.* P.O. Box 16004. Minneapolis, MN 55416, 1976.

21. Tinbergen, E. A. and N. *Autistic Children—New Hope for a Cure.* London: George Allen and Unwin, 1983.

OTHER PUBLICATIONS

22. Welch, Martha G. *Mother-Child Holding Therapy. More Than Just a Hug.* The Brown University Child Behavior and Development Letter. Vol 2, No. 13, 1986.

23. Welch, Martha G. *Toward Prevention of Developmental Disorders.* Pennsylvania Medicine. Vol. 9, No. 3, 1987.

VIDEOCASSETTES

1. *Kids in Motion.* Playhouse Video, Division of CBS/Fox Video, 39000 Seven Mile Road, Livonia, MI 48152. (A movement and exercise tape for children)

2. *Jane Fonda's New Workout Video.* Workout Institute, P.O. Box 2957, Beverly Hills, CA 90213. (A good exercise tape for adults)

3. *HOLDING TIME* Videocassette (VHS). *Holding Time* Videocassette, 127 East 59th Street, New York, NY 10022.

ORGANIZATIONS

La Leche League (breast-feeding groups)
Natural-childbirth groups

INDEX

ABOUT THE AUTHOR

Martha G. Welch, M.D., a graduate of Columbia University College of Physicians and Surgeons, is a practicing psychiatrist specializing in child development and parent-child attachment. Internationally renowned for her work on autism and mothering, in 1977 she founded The Mothering Center, which teaches *holding time* techniques to parents from all over the world. Dr. Welch lives in New York City and Greenwich, Connecticut, with her family. Her eight-year-old son volunteered this testimony about *holding time:* "After holding you feel as though you have never been angry and you never will be."

(203)
661-1413

Bryna Siegel
UCSF
DSM-III